*The Philosophical Principles
of Integral Knowledge*

The Philosophical Principles
of Integral Knowledge

Vladimir Solovyov

Translated by
Valeria Z. Nollan

WILLIAM B. EERDMANS PUBLISHING COMPANY
GRAND RAPIDS, MICHIGAN / CAMBRIDGE, U.K.

First published 1877 in Russian as *Filosofskie nachala tsel'nogo znaniia*

English translation © 2008 William B. Eerdmans Publishing Company
All rights reserved

Published 2008 by
Wm. B. Eerdmans Publishing Co.
2140 Oak Industrial Drive N.E., Grand Rapids, Michigan 49505 /
P.O. Box 163, Cambridge CB3 9PU U.K.

Library of Congress Cataloging-in-Publication Data

Solovyov, Vladimir Sergeyevich, 1853-1900.
The philosophical principles of integral knowledge / Vladimir Solovyov;
translated by Valeria Z. Nollan.
    p.   cm.
Includes bibliographical references and index.
ISBN 978-0-8028-6093-4 (pbk.: alk. paper)
1. Philosophy. I. Nollan, Valeria Z. II. Title.

B99.R92S6513   2008
197 — dc22

2008016823

www.eerdmans.com

*In memory of my father
Valentin Aleksandrovich Piven'
and my grandfather
Aleksandr Efimovich Piven'*

Contents

	Translator's Note	viii
	Acknowledgments	xi
	Translator's Introduction	1
Part I:	General Historical Introduction (concerning the Law of Historical Development)	19
Part II:	Concerning the Three Types of Philosophy	57
Part III:	Principles of Organic Logic: Characterization of Integral Knowledge — Point of Departure and Method of Organic Logic	75
Part IV:	Principles of Organic Logic (Continuation): Concept of the Absolute: Basic Definitions according to the Categories of the Existent, Essence, and Being	109
Part V:	Principles of Organic Logic (Continuation): Relative Categories That Define Idea as an Entity	139
	Appendix: Selected Works by V. S. Solovyov	169
	Notes	171
	Index	175

Translator's Note

Because of the creative and very particular nature of Solovyov's conceptual system, an explanation of some of the choices I have made as a translator may be helpful at the outset. Solovyov expresses what he affirms as the theosophical point of departure of organic logic through various terms: "that which is existent," "the existent," "the truly-existent," and "the absolutely-existent." All refer to the same concept. It may be worth mentioning as well that in almost all cases his understanding of truth is as eternal truth, which in Russian is истина *(istina)*, rather than the factual, everyday truth of правда *(pravda)*. This distinction is not readily apparent in the single word "truth" in English.

Some remarks need to be made concerning my translation of several philosophical terms that Solovyov uses in this treatise. When he has used the word категория, I have consistently translated it as "category." However, the word определение, which occurs throughout this text, can be translated appropriately as "category," "definition," or "characteristic." I considered carefully which of these meanings fits the sense at hand. In parts III and IV Solovyov manipulates concepts, principles, categories, definitions, characteristics, properties, and attributes, all of them in close and precise relationships within the schemes and systems he is establishing. He clearly is adapting the language and concepts of Hegelian organic logic and dialectics to his own speculative and highly imaginative philosophical system. Moreover, the terms and categories of nineteenth-century German idealist and metaphysical philosophy were still themselves not entirely fixed in their usage by various philosophers of that time. The reader will note that the title of part V reads Относительные категории, which I

Translator's Note

have translated literally as "Relative Categories." In the discussion that follows, however, Solovyov uses the word определение. I have intentionally chosen to use the word "characteristics" in the description of the concept of "idea," both because a characteristic can be understood as a more modest category and because this variety can approximate in English the rich linguistic store of words that is a feature of the Russian. It is probable that Solovyov distinguished between the larger concept of "category" (which seems stable in the Russian) and the more fluid one of определение. It is my hope that these choices will clarify, rather than confuse, the discussion in question.

In part V, in his discussion of idea as an entity, Solovyov introduces the terms то же and другое. The discussion interacts in some ways with Hegelian dialectics, in which the "self-other" juxtaposition occurs; it would be tempting to translate the two given Russian terms with these words. However, in part III of his treatise Solovyov elaborates his concept of "the existent in itself and of itself" as "the same entity, insofar as it does not relate to an other, i.e., in its own subjective reality." Thus I translate то же as "the same" and другое as "the other." The related term то же самое I render as "the identical one." I thank Boris Jakim for helping me to arrive at a workable rendering of these Solovyovian concepts.

An explanation of the system of notes in my translation is also in order. I have chosen to retain the endnotes provided in the text of the Academy of Sciences edition I used (which is faithful to the original publication), in the light of their helpfulness. Solovyov's own notes appear in this translation as footnotes in the same way in which they occur in his original text (these notes are designated by lowercased letters). In the event that I provide clarification, I do so with a footnote designated by an asterisk. On occasion I insert a helpful word or two in brackets in the text proper, to make absolutely precise some of the references that are unproblematic and obvious in the original Russian but that run the risk of becoming confused in an English translation. As much as is possible I avoid gender-specific language, not only in the spirit of fair-mindedness, but more importantly because of Solovyov's own progressive thinking concerning the status of women (one recalls his statement that "a woman is a person" and therefore has the capacity of any other human individual concerning intellectual activity).

Solovyov's enormous erudition is well known; in my translation I have retained the original words in French, German, English, Greek, and Latin that he used in his treatise. I have also tried to preserve as much as possible

TRANSLATOR'S NOTE

his original emphasis of key terms and phrases through italics and quotation marks. On several occasions I have divided his monstrously long paragraphs if I felt it would improve the readability of the translation. Similarly, I have broken some impossibly long sentences into two. I made these decisions with caution and in agony, since some of the original intonation may thus have been interrupted. The perfect, irreproachable translation is an ever-receding star on the horizon.

Acknowledgments

Any project involving Vladimir Solovyov's creative identity is deeply meaningful, and the current book is no exception. My translation of his *Филосовские начала цельного знания* (*The Philosophical Principles of Integral Knowledge*) was facilitated by institutions and individuals whose help was invaluable to me. I owe an enormous debt to the faculty and administration of Rhodes College: two Faculty Development Grants enabled me to conduct research in the Solovyov archives of the National Library of Russia at St. Petersburg. In addition, the Global Partners program of the Associated Colleges of the Midwest awarded me two grants that helped to advance my research on this book.

The collegiality and friendship of a number of individuals both in the United States and in Russia nourished my work throughout its various stages. I owe a special debt to Boris Jakim, whose expertise in Russian religious philosophy and warmhearted encouragement were invaluable to me. My deepest gratitude goes to Alexandra Kostina, who patiently went over many problematic Russian passages with me. I thank Tina Barr, Robert Bird, Jennifer Brady, Edith Clowes, Caryl Emerson, Tom Giacoponello, Brynn Keith, Judith Kornblatt, Michelle Mattson, Fr. Veniamin (Novik), Markus Pott, Sergei Sapunov, Paul Valliere, and Katheryn Wright for their inspiration. David Sick provided valuable assistance with Solovyov's numerous references in Greek and Latin. The expert typing of Carrie Wieners and Angela Kornman cheered me during the final stages of the project. Finally, I am grateful for the love and support of Richard and Alexander Nollan.

Translator's Introduction

The Importance of Solovyov's Philosophy for the Modern World

The arrival of the third millennium represents a fitting time for a reconsideration of the philosophy of Vladimir Sergeevich Solovyov, not only because the year 2000 marked the centennial of Solovyov's death, but also because of the enduring relevance and freshness of his philosophical ideas for world culture. Because of the growing realization in the West that Russian religious philosophy contains vast, untapped riches, the translation of Solovyov's corpus of works has proceeded rapidly. The current book aims to contribute to this worthwhile effort in offering the first translation into English of the philosopher-poet's treatise *Filosofskie nachala tsel'nogo znaniia* (1877).[1] Solovyov lived from 1853 to 1900; the writings he produced during his short life dramatically influenced the course of nineteenth- and twentieth-century Russian philosophical thought, and helped to lay the foundations for Russian Symbolist poetry (part of the Silver Age of Russian literature, 1880-1920). His works continue to influence contemporary religious philosophy, especially that of Russia, France, and Germany. His

---

1. *Filosofskie nachala tsel'nogo znaniia* (The philosophical principles of integral knowledge) was first published in *Zhurnal Ministerstva Narodnogo Prosveshcheniia*, 1877, vol. 190, no. 3, sec. II, pp. 60-99; no. 4, pp. 235-53; vol. 191, no. 6, pp. 199-233; vol. 193, no. 10, pp. 79-109; vol. 194, no. 11, pp. 1-32. I consulted these journals at the National Library of Russia, St. Petersburg. For my translation I used the following edition of the work: Vladimir Sergeevich Solov'ev, *Sochineniia v dvukh tomakh*, ed. A. V. Gulyga and A. F. Losev (Moscow: Akademiia nauk, Mysl', 1988). The text in this edition follows that of the original faithfully, except for its use of post-1917 Russian orthography.

most influential writings include *The Spiritual Foundations of Life* (1884), *Russia and the Universal Church* (1889), and *The Justification of the Good* (1897).[2] He knew the writers Fedor Dostoevsky and Leo Tolstoy intimately, and his nephew S. M. Solovyov proposed that he was Dostoevsky's prototype for two brothers in *The Brothers Karamazov* (1881) — the rationalist Ivan and the devout, saintly Alesha.[3] Solovyov knew or corresponded actively with the leading intellectual and religious figures of late-nineteenth-century Russia and Europe (such as Mikhail Katkov, Ivan Aksakov, and Bishop Strossmeyer of Yugoslavia), and he traveled extensively in those regions. It is thus not surprising that he wrote for an educated audience, which included philosophers, theologians, writers, and other intellectuals of his time.

Solovyov's philosophy manifests a sophistication and nobility of spirit that issue in equal proportions from his family tradition of learnedness, his religious background, and his own highly principled and compassionate personality. In defense of his positions he musters a formidable arsenal: a philosophical logic grounded in the major classical and Western texts, knowledge of the history of world religions, an intimate understanding of Russian Orthodox theology and praxis, and the finely tuned sensibilities of a poet and critic. His theories are presented in a logical mode familiar to the Western tradition, but they are densely informed by how Orthodox Christianity conceives of ethics — as an admixture of love, faith, and practice, in which the spirit of the law is more important than a rigid legalism.[4]

Taken as a whole, Solovyov's philosophy offers a powerful defense of religion in both mystical *and* logical terms, while providing readers with a fascinating entry into the mind of a liberal Russian Orthodox philosopher-poet. In its formative stages, which include *The Philosophical Principles of Integral Knowledge,* his philosophy inherited and was informed by the positions articulated by the Slavophiles during and after the Great Debates of

---

2. See the appendix for a more complete listing of Solovyov's works.

3. S. M. Solov'ev, *Vladimir Solov'ev: zhizn' i tvorcheskaia èvoliutsiia* (Moscow: Respublika, 1997), p. 180. The critical biography was written in 1922-23. It has been translated into English as follows: Sergey M. Solovyov, *Vladimir Solovyov: His Life and Creative Evolution,* trans. Aleksey Gibson, in 2 parts (Fairfax, Va.: Eastern Christian Publications, 2000).

4. See, in this connection, Vigen Guroian, *Incarnate Love: Essays in Orthodox Ethics* (Notre Dame, Ind.: University of Notre Dame Press, 1987), and John Polkinghorne, ed., *The Work of Love: Creation as Kenosis* (Grand Rapids: Eerdmans, 2001).

Translator's Introduction

the 1840s.⁵ Indeed, *The Philosophical Principles of Integral Knowledge* locates Solovyov's views securely within those of the Slavophiles: for example, in part I of the treatise he describes Russia as a messianic force that is historically and culturally determined. As his philosophical ideas matured in the late 1870s and 1880s, however, they became less ideologically tendentious and more critical of overly zealous nationalist stances: Solovyov rejected what he termed the "one-sided exclusiveness" found in some strains of Slavophile writing. He increasingly focused on the universal: his ideas became uniquely his own and highly creative, yet remaining Russian-based and rooted in Judeo-Russian Orthodox theology.

The keystone of the grand philosophical project Solovyov crafted throughout his life was a universal Christian theology that would synthesize Eastern Orthodoxy, Roman Catholicism, and Protestantism. In this context Solovyov's concept of all-unity *(vseedinstvo)* emerges as especially relevant. The philosopher Nicolas Berdyaev describes some of the compelling features of this project: "[Solovyov] had a vision of the integrality, the all-embracing unity of the world, of the divine cosmos, in which there is no separation of the parts from the whole. . . . It was an intellectual and erotic intuition; it was a quest for the transfiguration of the world, and for the Kingdom of God."⁶ Solovyov was a speculative philosopher who sought unity and reconciliation in the system of integral knowledge he elaborated: In *The Philosophical Principles of Integral Knowledge* he rejected the Asian East because its despotism limited individual freedom, while he viewed the West in its elevation of rationality and suspicion of mysticism as disintegrating into chaos. Positioned between these two flawed civiliza-

---

5. The Great Debates of the 1840s were concerned with the articulation of Russia's role in nineteenth-century civilization by the so-called Slavophiles and Westernizers. In broad terms the Slavophiles argued for a role and mission for Russia that would be compatible with that country's organic development, with its own unique history and cultural/religious traditions. The Westernizers affirmed that Russia should integrate its culture and practices increasingly with those of western Europe, with which it shared many significant features. On their most conciliatory and profound levels, the views of both groups were not incompatible with each other.

6. Nicolas Berdyaev, *The Russian Idea,* trans. R. M. French, introduction by Alexander Vucinich (Boston: Beacon Press, 1962), p. 168. Berdyaev points out, "Of the Russian thinkers of the nineteenth century V. Solovëv was the most universal; his thought had sources in Slavophilism but he gradually withdrew from the Slavophiles, and when there was an orgy of nationalism among us in the year '80 [1880] he became a sharp critic of Slavophilism" (p. 71). See especially pp. 166-79 for an insightful presentation of Solovyov's identity and philosophy.

tions is Russia and its spiritual tradition as the harmonious path to a radiant future for humankind; however, one must bear in mind in this context that Solovyov's religio-philosophical scheme is not equivalent with canonical Orthodoxy, since he introduces into his system some features of other forms of religious thought and mysticism.[7]

Solovyov's importance for Russian intellectual history cannot be overestimated, while his contribution to belles lettres in the form of refined mystical poetry assures him a worthy place in Russian Silver Age literature as well. His mystical experiencing of the world found its way into both his philosophical arguments and his literary aesthetics, emphasizing the individual's yearning for and ultimate union with the feminine wisdom principle of the divine Sophia. Complex and multifaceted in nature, the eternal feminine represented by Sophia possessed for Solovyov a vivid, specific reality as well as a cosmic elusiveness.[8] Solovyov's conception of Sophia is saturated with metaphysical and abstract features, but it also engages the corporeal, carnal nature of human identity; Berdyaev notes, "behind this striving after the all-embracing unity there was hidden an ardent love for the beauty of the divine cosmos, to which he gives the name of Sophia."[9] This love for the principles of the eternal feminine connects with the incarnation in that it is concretized in the form of the search for a particular woman; Solovyov's Christian cosmology is characterized by this duality of the soul — a belief in God, but concomitantly a belief in the human being.[10] In this sense it is deeply compatible with Christian theology, in particular that of Orthodoxy: Christ was both fully divine and fully human.[11] Furthermore, Solovyov's image of the divine Sophia is strongly suggestive

---

7. Marina Kostalevsky, *Dostoevsky and Soloviev: The Art of Integral Vision* (New Haven: Yale University Press, 1997), pp. 10-11. In this section Kostalevsky discusses Solovyov's views with respect to those of the Slavophiles Aleksei Khomiakov and Ivan Kireevsky.

8. See Boris Jakim and Laury Magnus, *Vladimir Solovyov's Poems of Sophia* (New Haven: Variable Press, 1996), and Judith Deutsch Kornblatt, "On Laughter and Vladimir Solov'ev's *Three Encounters*," *Slavic Review* 57, no. 3 (Fall 1998): 563-84.

9. Berdyaev, *The Russian Idea*, p. 168.

10. Berdyaev, *The Russian Idea*, pp. 97, 172.

11. For a relevant discussion on how Orthodox Christianity emphasizes in its theology the corporeality of Christ, developed in Solovyov's philosophy as the *bogochelovek* (divine-human being), see Alexandar Mihailovic, *Corporeal Words: Mikhail Bakhtin's Theology of Discourse* (Evanston, Ill.: Northwestern University Press, 1997), pp. 7-16, 140-42. These pages present an examination of the concepts of *perichoresis* (interpenetration) and enfleshment (embodiment).

Translator's Introduction

of classical beauty: a harmonious, pleasing form and a morally unimpeachable content draw the one contemplating such perfection to greater aesthetic and spiritual heights. Berdyaev framed the interconnectedness in Solovyov's writings of rationalism, Christian mysticism, and the Platonic ideal of beauty in the following description:

> [T]here was a Soloviev of the day and the Soloviev of the night, outwardly revealing himself, and in that very revelation concealing himself, and in the most important aspect not revealing himself at all. Only in his poetry has he revealed what was hidden, what was veiled and overwhelmed by the rational schemes of his philosophy. . . . He was a mystic; he had a mystical experience. . . . He was an erotic philosopher in the Platonic sense of the word. *Eros* of the highest order played an immense part in his life and was his existential theme; and at the same time there was a strong ethical element in him; he demanded the effective realization of Christian morality in the whole of life.[12]

When one considers the broad-ranging areas of thought that Solovyov's philosophy embraces, along with his appreciation of mysticism, it is easy to understand his appeal to various intellectuals and traditions seemingly incompatible with each other.[13] Both right- and left-wing intellectuals considered his voice a leading one in the discourse on Russia's future; his deep admiration for Judaism won him the respect of leaders of that faith tradition; and his elevation of some features of Roman Catholicism enabled him to foster significant connections with theologians of Western Christianity throughout his life.

Because Solovyov is widely acknowledged as Russia's most important religious philosopher and a first-rate poet, a familiarity with his writings will enable readers to understand the distinctive perspectives on world religions and European philosophy held by a thinker whose enormous erudition has been compared to that of Saint Thomas Aquinas. An understanding of Solovyov's philosophical system will illuminate the ways in which Russian Orthodox theology has evolved within its own canon, and can reveal the ways in which its sensibilities differ from those of the Western Christian confessions. Solovyov's philosophy contributed a liberal and more modern (as opposed to the traditional patristic) stream to Russian

---

12. Berdyaev, *The Russian Idea*, pp. 167-68.
13. Berdyaev, *The Russian Idea*, pp. 166-67.

Orthodox thought.[14] In broader terms, Solovyov's provocative and persuasive ideas contribute to the body of work known as the "Russian idea"; his article "The Russian Idea" ("Russkaia ideia," 1888) was foundational in outlining the parameters of this concept. A close acquaintance with his works will lead to a more accurate conceptualization of the issues of the Great Debates, which constitute a major component of the Russian idea. These debates fermented throughout the nineteenth and twentieth centuries, reemerging in the latter century in the ideological polemics between the Russian nationalists and the internationalists. Solovyov's writings thus enable us to understand contemporary Russian nationalism in its broadminded and Christian iterations; his thought, in its interaction with the prevailing intellectual currents of his day, also helps us to appreciate tensions and divergences within Russian nationalism as such. The material of Solovyov's life, his body of poetry, and his writings on aesthetics provide valuable insights into some essential features of the Russian national identity: the distinctiveness of life on Russian country estates and the culture it produced, the connections between czarist monarchism and Russian Orthodoxy, and the particular breadth of spirit that is nurtured by the geography of Russia's steppes and open plains.[15] Perhaps most importantly, a familiarity with Solovyov's life and works will illuminate for those with an abiding interest in world culture the enigmatic and distinctive qualities of the Russian religious mind.

The Philosophical Principles of Integral Knowledge

Solovyov's foundational treatise *The Philosophical Principles of Integral Knowledge* represents the earliest elaboration of the major ideas that would occupy him throughout his life, and as such it is of considerable importance for an accurate understanding of how his philosophical positions were initially formulated. Completed in 1874 when Solovyov was only

---

14. For a thorough exposition and analysis of the "two streams of Russian theological thought," the neo-patristic and the Russian schools, see Paul Valliere, *Modern Russian Theology: Bukharev, Soloviev, Bulgakov* (Edinburgh: T. & T. Clark, 2000), esp. pp. 1-15.

15. For a persuasive discussion of the relationship between Russians and the landscape of their country — the psychology of geography — see Dmitrii S. Likhachev, *Reflections on Russia*, trans. Christina Sever, ed. Nicolai N. Petro (Boulder, Colo.: Westview Press, 1991), pp. 16-23, 174-79.

twenty-four, the treatise outlines key concepts of his philosophical system — theosophy, theocracy, and theurgy — within the overarching framework of integral knowledge, understood by Solovyov as attainable in the "true philosophy" that connects humankind with the "absolute first principle of existence," with the eternal kingdom of God.[16] Displaying Solovyov's incisive powers of analysis and possessing a youthful vitality, the treatise breaks off abruptly in part V. While working on this book the philosopher-poet also began the *Critique of Abstract Principles* (1877-80). For reasons that are not entirely clear, Solovyov abandoned the idea of submitting *The Philosophical Principles* as his dissertation and decided to replace it with the *Critique of Abstract Principles*.[17]

The Philosophical Principles of Integral Knowledge is characterized by a rigorous exegesis; a broad consideration of historical, religious, and philosophical ideas; the insertion of poetry to illustrate and deepen the meaning of a particular statement; and a self-confidence born of a thorough study of the relevant texts and intellectual movements to buttress the author's arguments. Solovyov's perspicacity remains impressive in his analysis of enormous amounts of historical and religious information. S. M. Solovyov, the philosopher's nephew, writes this about the book: "This work was written brilliantly; some of the ideas in it were not repeated in his [Solovyov's] later works or are expressed in them in a weaker form."[18] Moreover, as S. M. Solovyov continues, the work "represents the connecting link between the 'Sophia' of Cairo [1875] and *Lectures on Godmanhood* [1877-81]."[19] Indeed, in Solovyov's writings the insertion of poetry, both his own and that of other poets, remains a distinctive feature. This practice supports the claim that all genres of his writing contributed to what ultimately must be considered an integrity and an *integrality* of thought. The philosopher-poet would agree that integral knowledge comes in a variety of modes, including the philosophical and the poetic. In his biography of his uncle, S. M. Solovyov quotes V. S. Solovyov: "Since poetry and metaphysics are characteristic only of man, he can be defined as a poeticizing and metaphysicizing animal."[20]

---

16. Berdyaev, *The Russian Idea*, p. 168.

17. S. M. Solov'ev, *Vladimir Solov'ev: zhizn' i tvorcheskaia èvoliutsiia*, p. 133.

18. S. M. Solov'ev, *Vladimir Solov'ev: zhizn' i tvorcheskaia èvoliutsiia*, p. 133, translation VN.

19. S. M. Solov'ev, *Vladimir Solov'ev: zhizn' i tvorcheskaia èvoliutsiia*, pp. 133-34.

20. Sergei M. Lukianov, *Materialy k biografii Solov'eva*, vols. 1-3 (Petrograd, 1916-21), 1:7; quoted in Sergey M. Solovyov, *Vladimir Solovyov*, part I, p. 105.

TRANSLATOR'S INTRODUCTION

A summary of the central ideas in *The Philosophical Principles of Integral Knowledge* is presented below; special attention is given to the longer first chapter, in which Solovyov's frame of reference and "global concepts" are introduced.

Part I: General Historical Introduction
(concerning the Law of Historical Development)

Solovyov introduces his treatise with a clarification of its intent, namely, to address in philosophical discourse the purpose of human existence. He states that this question is engaged by each individual first in *personal* terms, and subsequently in the context of the individual's interaction with others in various social spheres. The purpose of existence becomes personal, social, and ultimately universal; it is understood in the loftiest metaphysical and teleological terms. Solovyov seeks to explicate no less than the common and final goal of human existence, by which a human life acquires nobility and meaning. After presenting the concept of human development by scientific analogy to the development of biological organisms, the philosopher explores the features that define a person's nature. He calls these features "three basic forms of being": feeling (with the goal of objective beauty), thinking (with the goal of objective truth), and active will (with the goal of objective good).

Solovyov examines the latter feature of human nature, active will, first in his treatise. Will is defined as "the first spontaneous principle of social life," and occurs in three stages: economic society, political society, and spiritual or sacred society. A person desires, respectively, material existence, lawful existence, and absolute or eternal existence. At this early point in Solovyov's essay it is already clear not only which direction his argument will take, but also that he intends to engage and reconceptualize Hegel's ideas on human development: As the purpose of human existence and development, only the last stage (since Solovyov makes clear that the three stages must be understood as progressing from lowest to highest in significance) can satisfy humankind's yearning for absolute, integral knowledge. Only that level of understanding, both reasonable and mystical, of the interconnectedness of all things in a Christian cosmological context, is worthy of philosophical inquiry.

Next Solovyov turns to thinking or knowledge, similarly separating

8

Translator's Introduction

this activity of the human being into three graded areas: empirical or positive science, abstract philosophy, and theology. It is noteworthy that in his philosophical universe mysticism and religion remain fully legitimate and unmarked components of reality, inseparable from the other aspects of a person's experiencing of existence. Thus the keystone of his philosophical system is theology, which provides other, "lower" types of knowledge with an absolute positive content and an ultimate, universal goal.

Finally, Solovyov examines the sphere of feelings, but not in the subjective, personal sense; rather, his interest lies in the general meaning of subjective expression, i.e., in the elucidation of the meaning of artistic creation and the search for beauty. Paradigmatically with the spheres of active will and knowledge, he underscores the inextricable link between the personal and the absolute/Divine: a person's creation "necessarily presupposes a perception of the highest creative powers in feeling" (p. 30 note e).[21] In this sphere as well Solovyov keeps the focus of his treatise on the concept of a higher world apprehended through mystical experience, defining mysticism appropriately as "[t]he creative relationship of human feeling to this transcendental world" (p. 31).

Early in part I Solovyov presents the relationships among the aforementioned categories synoptically in the following table:

	I Sphere of Creation	II Sphere of Knowledge	III Sphere of Practical Activity
Subjective basis	feeling	thinking	will
Objective principle	beauty	truth	common good
1st level: absolute	Mysticism	Theology	Spiritual society (church)
2nd level: formal	Fine art	Abstract philosophy	Political society (the state)
3rd level: material	Technical applied art	Positive science	Economic society (the *zemstvo*)

Based on his discussion of the categories, in all three spheres level 1/the absolute represents the most profound for individual and social develop-

---

21. Page numbers that appear in parentheses in this introduction refer to the present book.

ment. Most importantly, "preeminent significance belongs to the sphere of creation" (p. 32).

After establishing the basic categories of his initial conceptual scheme, Solovyov applies them to the evolution of history from antiquity to his own late-nineteenth-century times. He concludes that in antiquity there was no differentiation among economic, political, and spiritual societies: Each sphere was connected with the other two, while theology, philosophy, science, and art were inextricably bound up with each other. The unity among theology, philosophy, and science Solovyov calls "theosophy"; church, government, and economic society become a "theocracy"; and mysticism, fine art, and technical art converge as a "theurgy." He defines integral knowledge as the final result of a free theosophy, a state of being arrived at freely and not coerced.

Solovyov continues with one of his decisive propositions: Only with the origins of Christianity did a genuine freedom from a false unity emerge — the sacred was differentiated from the profane in society and human existence in general:

> In reality, once the Christian church designated itself as the only spiritual, sacred society, considering everything else to be *profanum*, by this very act it took away the government's entire previous significance — it repudiated the sacred republic. In recognizing the government solely as a restraining, repressive force, Christians stripped it of any positive spiritual content.... This relationship negated the very principle of ancient society, which entailed specifically the deification of the republic and the emperor as its representative, the merging of spiritual and secular principles. Hence the emperors, in persecuting the Christians, were acting not as bearers of governmental powers in the narrow sense of the term (Christianity was not threatening this power at all), but as bearers of the entire ancient consciousness. (pp. 35-36)

Arriving in his analysis at the time of Constantine the Great, Solovyov points out that two "heterogeneous social forms, the church and the state," served as organizing principles for civilization. He concludes that because in the East the state subordinated the church to its control but lacked a deeper legitimacy, it "fell along with the Eastern Church to Islam" (p. 37). By contrast, in the West the church (represented by Roman Catholicism) and the secular Germanic state remained at odds with each other.

Translator's Introduction

The Middle Ages ushered in a transition from the unifying force of Roman Catholicism (described by Solovyov as "the Roman ecclesiastical state") to the far-reaching Protestant Reformation. However, he does not offer Protestantism as the model for an integrated ecclesiastical system: his Slavophile views come into play as he rejects both the Asian/Islamic and the Western Christian models. Solovyov especially dismisses positivism and materialist socialism in the West as potential sources for the meaning of human existence; one recalls the full title of his *Critique of Abstract Principles: Against the Positivists*. His argument in *The Philosophical Principles of Integral Knowledge* moves from a position of categorical rejection of the secular West to that of ecstatic joy upon recalling the wellsprings of meaning and purpose for humanity:

> [T]he final results of Western civilization in their narrowness and shallowness can satisfy only the corresponding narrow and shallow minds and hearts. As long as religious sensibility and philosophical inquiry exist in humankind, as long as humankind retains its aspiration for the eternal and ideal, mysticism, pure art, theology, metaphysics, and the church will remain undefeatable, notwithstanding all the successes and claims of the lower levels [of vulgar artistic currents — VN], whose champions are only a mental and moral *vulgus*.[22] (p. 48)

In comparing the Islamic East with Western civilization, Solovyov determines that the former is in some important ways "higher" than the latter because of its unity and internal spiritual content (as opposed to the West's "complete anarchy or headlessness"). He posits a third stage, a "new historic force" (the Slavic peoples), whose task "will consist of revitalizing

---

22. Solovyov's rejection of the values of the secular West may seem unduly harsh, but they were by no means unusual for his time. One notes Dostoevsky's assessment of the West, through his character Ivan Karamazov in *The Brothers Karamazov* (1881), as a "precious cemetery." The young Solovyov's intellectual development was nourished on the views of such seminal Slavophile thinkers as Ivan Kireevsky (1806-56), to wit: "Our final goal is an enlightenment which is incompatible with the one-sided enlightenment of the West and which completely meets the needs of the living, reasoning spirit. . . . The Western peoples have closed the circle of their development and have attained a one-sided maturity. . . . Russia is capable of leading Europe out of her moral torpor, if she first can absorb West European enlightenment" (quoted from A. G. Lushnikov, *I. V. Kireevskii. Ocherk zhizni i religiozno-filosofskogo mirovozzreniia* [Kazan': n.p., 1913], in Vladimir Soloukhin, *A Time to Gather Stones*, trans. Valerie Z. Nollan [Evanston, Ill.: Northwestern University Press, 1993], 177).

and spiritualizing the elements that are hostile and lifeless . . . by means of higher conciliatory principles, and of giving them a common, absolute content, by which they will be freed of exclusive self-affirmation and mutual negation" (p. 50). Consistently in his philosophical scheme Solovyov underscores that this process will be voluntary and "free": "Only the kind of theology that is grounded in independent philosophy and science may . . . be transformed into free theosophy, since only those who grant freedom to others are free themselves" (p. 53). He concludes part I of his treatise by offering the hope for a future "single integral organism," a free theocracy or integral society.

Part II: Concerning the Three Types of Philosophy

Solovyov begins this section of his treatise with a consideration of "free theosophy," which he defines as a synthesis of theology, philosophy, and experimental science. He affirms that *only* this synthesis may contain the integral truth of knowledge. Without such a synthesis the given areas of thought exist only in separateness, insufficiently developed, isolated from the interconnected whole that for Solovyov forms eternal and absolute truth. What concerns him here is philosophical thought as his point of departure: he maintains that "genuine philosophy" must have a theosophical character.

Solovyov continues to develop his argument with a consideration of the origins and various meanings of the concept of "philosophy." Two historically significant conceptions of philosophy are: as a theory only for academic circles, and as a matter for life as well as for academic circles. (The second conception Solovyov would develop in his essay "Plato's Life Drama" ["Zhiznennaia drama Platona," 1898], which defined the struggles of the Greek philosopher's life and work.) For Solovyov the essential meaning of the term "philosophy" resides in the Greek word φιλοσοφία, love of wisdom — this concept encompasses the fullness of knowledge, moral perfection, and an inner wholeness of spirit.

Solovyov elaborates the particular content of the three major currents of philosophy — mysticism, rationalism, and empiricism — indicating that the latter two are incomplete without mysticism. He attaches the highest, "preeminent" significance to mysticism, considering it to define "the supreme principle and final goal of philosophical knowledge" (p. 72).

Translator's Introduction

Solovyov's argument assumes that earlier forms of philosophical inquiry and practice have not attained a true "integral knowledge" because of their evolution in human history away from integrality and into, as he puts it, one-sided and narrow conceptualizations. He calls for a fuller development and synthesis of the broadest and most crucial areas of thought: If positive science, philosophy, and theology can all be freed of their historically narrow and limited meanings, they will all become the higher concept of "free theosophy." The philosopher continues, "If the latter [free theosophy] is generally defined as integral knowledge, in particular it must be designated as integral science or as integral philosophy; the difference here lies only in the point of departure and mode of elaboration, for the results and positive content are the same" (p. 57).

Solovyov states, "Empiricism allows the cognition only of phenomena," and a phenomenon exists only with respect to "us as the cognizing subject." From this standpoint he turns to the idealist and rationalist philosophical systems of Kant and Hegel, concentrating on the concept of absolute being. He is in search of the "truly-existent" (истинно-сущее), with respect to its positioning in the material world. He concludes that genuine truth, the realm of the truly-existent, "contains both its own reality and its own reasonableness, and superimposes these qualities onto everything else" (p. 70). This reality must include mysticism, that which is supramaterial, metaphysical. Solovyov points out, however, that mystical knowledge may be only *the basis* for genuine philosophy, but that it is *necessary*, since without it the philosophy of empiricism and rationalism contains "false principles" and "absurd conclusions" (p. 71).

Part III: Principles of Organic Logic: Characterization of Integral Knowledge — Point of Departure and Method of Organic Logic

In this section Solovyov characterizes organic logic by describing its deep semantic meanings: the concept is related to integral knowledge or free theosophy (it is organic) and it is a logical system (it is logical). With respect to its connection to theosophical knowledge, Solovyov identifies seven "points of departure": the subject of cognition, the goal, the general material, the form, the generative cause of cognition, the point of departure itself, and the method of its development. He considers the first five points of departure, or "relationships," together, because their philosophical interconnectedness lends itself to a focus on the all-important subject of free theosophy. This subject represents the heart of Solovyov's metaphysical and mystical search: the "truly-existent." It is the subject specifically of free theosophy, which, as the philosopher reminds us, encompasses the entire objective content of empiricism, rationalism, and mysticism. Solovyov reiterates that the "goal of genuine philosophy is . . . to promote a person's internal union with the truly-existent" (p. 78). Here we encounter evidence of Solovyov's consistency of thought concerning genuine philosophy as a search for the knowledge of truth: this truth is linked both with creative work (truth must reside in an aesthetic form of the material world) and with moral activity (truth must be manifested in real-life actions). He would refine these thoughts further in the essays "Beauty in Nature" ("Krasota v prirode," 1889) and "The Universal Meaning of Art" ("Obshchii smysl iskusstva," 1890). Beauty is the aesthetic material, the form that provides a conduit for the vital content of goodness and truth. Thus our understanding of our connection with the truly-existent, with a higher, absolute realm of spirituality, and with a moral order is dependent on material nature. Solovyov concludes that mystical phenomena (as possessing primary importance), "[t]he sphere of physical being . . . and the psychic sphere . . . are indisputably necessary for the fullness of absolute being" (pp. 81-82).

In his search for a satisfying characterization of general, objective cognition, Solovyov examines the Hegelian concept of the *Ding an sich* (thing-in-itself) and the German philosopher's understanding of reality, as well as the Kantian categories of the mind; he affirms that this integral type of cognition "must combine the reality of sensory perception with universal community and the necessity of the a priori form" (p. 94). Solovyov discusses the nature of being (primarily with respect to the Hegelian system), concluding that the "absolute first principle," which makes cognition general and represents the principle of Solovyovian organic logic, is "that which is existent" (the truly-existent), and not being.

Concerning the remaining two characteristics (the point of departure and the method) of the seven that form the subject of part III, Solovyov concludes his discussion with references to organic logic's point of departure being the concept (λόγος) of the absolute first principle, while the method may be only "pure dialectical thinking," which (as Solovyov defines it) from a general principle produces a concrete content. Solovyov

Translator's Introduction

envisions this content as evolving continuously into an "ideal organism," thus establishing the suitability of this system and method for organic logic and integral knowledge.

Part IV: Principles of Organic Logic (Continuation): Concept of the Absolute: Basic Definitions according to the Categories of the Existent, Essence, and Being

Solovyov continues his elaboration of organic logic by tackling some fundamental categories of philosophy, and recasting them to integrate them more coherently into his own religio-philosophical system. At all times he is concerned with an individual person's integral existence, rather than differentiated experience. He states that integral knowledge must have both a theoretical and a practical character, that it must "satisfy . . . all the highest aspirations of a person" (p. 109). He first considers the interrelationship between the concepts of the absolute and the existent with respect to being, underscoring that the genuine absolutely-existent contains in itself "all of being and all realities" (p. 112). He reminds the reader of the positioning of the absolute itself with respect to various philosophical systems: In its separateness from everything it is defined *negatively* with respect to this everything, while in its possessing of everything and in not having anything outside of itself it is defined *positively*. The absolutely-existent of Solovyov's "first theosophical science" (p. 112) is required by human reason, feeling, and will.

Solovyov evolves his discussion of the aforementioned categories into a consideration of the absolute as containing both itself and its other (an other), as comprising a unity of itself and its opposite. Here he provides glimpses of the way he would characterize (sexual) love between a man and woman in his later, profoundly insightful essay "The Meaning of Love" ("Smysl liubvi," 1892). Love for Solovyov is conceptualized in a way that is conscious of and compatible with Russian Orthodox theology: love is conceived as an ascetic and kenotic act, a rejection of the egotism accompanying the separate self, as well as the creation (in the process of merging emotionally and physically) of a new and integrated being that contains a vital connective spark to divinity and immortality.

Continuing his discussion of philosophical categories, Solovyov examines analogously the relationships among: the existent, essence, being;

might, necessity, reality; God, idea, and nature. He concretizes somewhat the discussion in this section, offering examples, such as "my thinking as a characteristic of my personal being" and "the content . . . of my particular thinking" as representing two different meanings of the concept of "being" (pp. 120-21). Thus he designates the second connotation, of the content of thinking, as a category of "essence," to distinguish it from the first, which he designates as "being." He further particularizes his discussion of the existent, essence, and being by identifying "an original distinction in the existent itself" (p. 121) in the "first center," which he defines as "the self-affirmation of the absolutely-existent, or God." This for Solovyov represents the crux of the matter, the philosopher's search for meaning in a concretized self positioned in eternal time in such a way as to experience a moral and emotionally whole positive self-affirmation with respect to the overcoming of mortality and the attainment of eternal existence. He consequently elaborates the three principles of the "supreme Trinity": the Kabbalistic En-Sof, Logos, and the Holy Spirit. Solovyov brings his discussion of the various categories to a close by returning to the all-important connection between the existent and Idea as a mode of being that is desired (will), imagined (knowledge), and felt (feeling). He summarizes that the existent, "in affirming the idea as the good, gives it by means of truth manifestations in beauty" (p. 135).

Part V: Principles of Organic Logic (Continuation): Relative Categories That Define Idea as an Entity

The last part of Solovyov's treatise is unfinished.[23] He undertakes to clarify the fullness of the relationships existing within the concept of Logos: it is "the relationship of the superexistent to its own self" (differentiated within itself) and "the relationship of the superexistent to everything and of everything to the superexistent" (because the superexistent is the absolute). Solovyov identifies three Logoi: the internal or concealed Logos, the revealed Logos, and the embodied or concrete Logos. All three are perfectly interrelated. Concerning the third, the embodied or concrete Logos,

---

23. In my discussion of part V of *The Philosophical Principles of Integral Knowledge*, I am indebted to the fine and comprehensive presentation of its contents by S. M. Solovyov, *Vladimir Solovyov,* part I, chapter 6, esp. pp. 179-80.

Translator's Introduction

Solovyov affirms its correspondence to the "concrete idea or Sophia." He evolves the concept of Sophia from patristic philosophy and especially from Origen, but notes that he will focus on the first two Logoi, leaving a more thorough discussion of Sophia for a later time.

Solovyov subsequently outlines the categories of the existent, essence, and being as concepts that belong to the absolute, Logos, and Idea, but in different ways. He considers the following relationships:

(1) the Existent *(Absolute)*	(2) Being *(Logos)*	(3) Essence *(Idea)*
1. the Absolute ... Spirit	Will	the Good
2. Logos .... Mind	Imagination	Truth
3. Idea .... Soul	Feeling	Beauty

He concentrates on the description of Idea, pointing out that as the "manifested absolute," Idea is the "*realized unity ... unity in everything* or in multiplicity" (p. 142). Idea in Solovyov's cosmological system integrates spirit, mind, and soul. He clarifies that these states of being are "substantially unified in the absolute, differentiated in Logos, and unite actually in Idea" (p. 143). The entire fullness of Divinity can be discerned in Idea, in which the three aspects of truth, good, and beauty converge.

Solovyov then discusses relative characteristics organized according to the categories of entity, organism, and person. He utilizes Hegelian dialectics in presenting the specific binaries that are resolved in a third term, which represents Idea as the expression of truth. Among these binaries are "the same" and "the other," which equate as and are resolved into "something." He rejects the type of philosophy that manipulates logical definitions not as predicates of the existent, but wholly as abstract forms that are completely freestanding and independent in their abstractness. He is concerned about particularity, integratedness, and the law of identity as necessary components of a viable philosophical system. As part of his discussion, he mounts a critique not only of Kant and Hegel (whose categories and systems possess, in his view, a relative rather than an unconditional character), but also, through linguistic analysis, of the limitations of French and English philosophy. At this point Solovyov's discussion ends.

Even though Solovyov was deeply disappointed at the end of his life that his religio-philosophical program for humankind's spiritual viability was not gaining currency in Russia, he never abandoned the *ideals* or the *foundational concepts* he articulated so eloquently and consistently throughout his philosophical career. He understood that the majestic principles of all-unity, integral knowledge arrived at through both earthly and mystical experience, and Sophia — the ideal of wisdom and beauty — would remain worthy of further investigation and perhaps would bring radiant joy for the best minds that would succeed him in the future.

Valeria Z. Nollan

PART I

General Historical Introduction
(concerning the Law of Historical Development)

The first question that any philosophy claiming to be of general interest should answer is the question of the purpose of [human] existence. If our existence were a state of uninterrupted bliss, then such a question could not arise: our blissful existence would be its own goal and would not require any explanation. But since in reality bliss exists more in the imagination (reality consists of a series of major and minor torments, and in the happiest case is, on the one hand, a constant alternation between hard work and oppressive boredom and, on the other hand, a series of disappearing illusions), the question emerges entirely of its own volition: What does all of this mean? What is the purpose of this life? The question arises for each thinking individual first in *personal* terms, as a question concerning the goal of his own existence. But since, on the one hand, all thinking beings are approximately in the same situation with respect to this question, and since, on the other hand, each being can exist only in interaction with the others, so that the goal of one person's life is indissolubly linked with the goals of other people's lives, the personal question necessarily is transformed into a general one: What is the goal of human existence in general? For what reason, to what end does humankind exist? Our consciousness demands a common and final goal, because it is clear that the dignity of the personal and immediate goals of a human life can define itself only by its relationship to that *common* and *final* goal for which it serves as the means. In this regard, if we take away the latter, then our immediate goals also lose their entire value and meaning, and we are left with only the innate impulses of a primitive animal nature.

If we, in leaving the unstable soil of popular opinion, turn to the objective investigation of our question, then first and foremost we must arrive at a clear awareness of *what* specifically is meant by the term "the universal goal" of humankind. This term necessarily presupposes another one, "development," and in emphasizing that humankind has the common goal of its existence, we must acknowledge that it *is developing*; if history did not constitute development, but rather the changing phenomena linked with each other merely in an external manner, then clearly it would not be possible to talk about any common goal whatsoever.

Since the beginning of the current century, the term "development" has become a part not only of scientific but also of colloquial thinking. This does not mean, however, that the logical content of this idea became completely accessible to the common consciousness; on the contrary, this content remains rather murky and undefined, and not only for the half-educated crowd that expounds in a pell-mell manner on development, but even on occasion for scholars and quasi philosophers who use this concept in their theoretical constructs. For this reason we should examine what is properly contained within the term "development," and what is presupposed by it.

First and foremost, development presupposes a specific subject, about which it can be said that it is developing: development presupposes a developing subject. This is completely self-evident, but nonetheless sometimes overlooked. Furthermore, an absolutely simple and isolated body of matter cannot be a subject that is developing, because absolute simplicity excludes the possibility of any kind of change, and consequently of development. In general, it is worth noting that the concept of an absolutely simple body of matter belonging to a scholastic dogmatism is not justified by philosophical criticism. But, on the other hand, a mechanical aggregate of elements or parts cannot be subject to development, either: the changes taking place in a granite cliff or a pile of sand cannot be called "development." And if what is subject to development cannot be an absolutely simple body of matter or a mechanical, external combination of elements, then it can be only a single being that contains in itself a multitude of elements that are internally connected to each other, i.e., *a living organism*. Indeed, only organisms can develop in the proper meaning of the word, and herein lies their essential distinction from the rest of nature. However, some changes in an organism do not promote its development. Such changes, in which the determining significance belongs to external agents that are foreign to the organism itself, may influence the external course of development, slow it down, or cause it to cease altogether, thereby destroying the subject. But these cannot be considered a part of development itself: Only those changes participate in it that have their root or source in the developing being itself, which issue from it, and only for their final manifestation, for their complete realization require an external stimulus. The material of development and the impelling source of its realization come from the outside, but this impelling source can act, it goes without saying, only in conjunction with the peculiar nature of the organism; i.e., it is determined in its action by the agency of this organism. In the same way, to remain as such the material of development must become like (be assimilated into) the organism itself, i.e., must assume its basic forms, and must be processed by the action of the organism for its own organic purposes, so that the method and content of the development are determined internally by the developing entity itself. In scholastic language, the external elements and agents produce only the *causam materialem* and *causam efficientem* (ἀρχὴ τῆς χινήσεος) of development; the *causa formalis* and *causa finalis* are contained in the subject of development itself.[1]

A series of changes without a known point of origin that continues indefinitely, not having any specific purpose, cannot be considered "development," since each component of such a series, in the absence of a common origin that determines its relative importance, could not constitute a definite stage of development; instead, it would remain merely an undifferentiated change. If, as noted above, the concept of a goal presupposes the idea of development, then likewise the latter necessarily requires the former. Consequently, *development is that series of immanent changes in an organic being that proceeds from a known origin and directs itself toward a known, definite goal*: such is the development of every organism; *endless development* is simply nonsense, *contradictio in adjecto*. Thus we must assume three common, necessary stages of any type of development: a known primary condition, from which it is initiated; another known condition, which is its goal; and a series of intermediate conditions, as a transition or means, since if there were no resulting or gradual transition from the first to the last stage they would merge into each other, and we would not have any development at all, but only a single undifferentiated state. The general formula that expresses these three stages is the *law of development*. When we define the law of development, we also define its purpose. This is not to say that the law and the purpose are one and the same, but a knowledge of the first also gives us knowledge of the second: Hence, if we know the law according to which a plant develops, then we also know the purpose of this development — the production of fruit — as the last stage of progressive change that is determined by this law.

If development is an immanent process that uses external data only as a stimulus and as a material, then all the determining origins and composite elements of development must already exist in the primary state of the organism — the bud. This is actually proven by the fact that from the seed of a known plant or the embryo of a known animal it is impossible to produce anything other than this particular kind of plant or animal. Thus the primary state of an organism, or its bud, in its composite elements, is already a *complete organism,* and if in this way the distinction between the bud and the fully developed organism cannot consist of the difference between the constitutive origins and elements themselves, then it clearly must be found in the distinction contained within its *state* or *arrangement.* And if in a developed organism the composite elements and forms are arranged in such a way that each has its definite place and function, the primary, or embryonic, state manifests the opposite quality: in it the composite forms and elements of the organism do not yet have their strictly determined place and function — in other words, they are mixed, undifferentiated. Their distinction presents itself as unexpressed, hidden, existing only potentially. They have not become separate, have not manifested their distinctiveness, have not become detached. In this manner, development must properly consist of the separation or detachment of the composite forms and elements of an organism in the light of their new, already fully organic combination. If in fact *new* composite forms and elements do not have to enter into the development from outside, then it clearly may consist only of changes in its state or the arrangement of elements *already present* in it. The first state is a mixture or external unity; here the components of an organism are linked with each other purely by external means. In the third, perfected state they are linked with each other internally and freely, in accordance with their own function, and they support and complement each other by virtue of their internal solidarity. This presupposes, however, their prior detachment or isolation, since they could not have entered into an internal, free union as independent components of an organism, if at an earlier point they had not received this independence through differentiation upon becoming isolated, which constitutes the second major stage of development. It is not difficult to show the necessity of the transition from the second to the third state.

Concerning the Law of Historical Development

The isolation of each formative element is inextricably linked with the urge to drive out all the others, to destroy them as something separate or make them a part of its own material; since this urge is similarly intrinsic to each element, they all counterbalance each other. But a simple equilibrium would be possible only if all the forming elements were completely alike, and this cannot happen in an organism. In fact, with complete similarity of elements each one could receive from all the others only what it already possesses, in which case there would decidedly be no basis for their tight internal union. Only a purely mechanical, accidental union would be possible, forming an aggregate rather than an organism (thus the combination of similar grains of sand forms a pile of sand, the accidental union of which falls apart with each external action). In this manner, each component in an organism possesses its own necessary distinction or specificity, and as a result the simple equilibrium necessarily leads here to a state in which each element counterbalances all the others not as a single unit in opposition to other units similar to itself, but in accordance with its own internal character and significance. Thus in a human organism the brain and heart have significance not as components equal to all the others, but in accordance with their own particular function, and fulfill the role of major organs that all the rest must serve for the preservation of the integrity of the entire organism, and consequently of themselves as well. It follows, then, that the necessary result is not a mechanical equilibrium, but rather an internal organic union, which constitutes in its complete realization the third major stage of development.

It is noteworthy that the undifferentiation of the first stage is only relative: an absolute undifferentiation cannot exist in an organism in any of its states. The particularities of the forming parts exist in the first stage of development as well, but they are tied to and overwhelmed by the element of unity, which in this case is characterized by an exceptional defining characteristic. In the second stage, on the contrary, this defining characteristic is transferred to the separate components and the previous element of unity itself becomes merely one of the many components (in this way, for example, the Catholic Church, which at the beginning of the Middle Ages was the only defining element of unity, in recent times has become merely one of the components in the common organism of civilization). In this second stage the connecting unity of all components becomes only an abstract force or general law, which takes on a living reality and becomes a concrete whole in the third stage.

Such is the general law of every type of development. Now we must apply it to a definite, known reality, specifically to the historical development of humankind.[a] The subject of development here is humankind as a real, albeit collective organism. Usually, when people talk about humankind as a single entity or organism, they see in this little more than a metaphor or simple abstraction: the significance of a single, real being, or individual, applies only to each separate person. But this is completely unfounded. The fact is that every being and every organism possess a necessarily collective character and the difference is one only of degree; clearly there can be no absolutely simple organism. Each individual being — this person, for example — is made up of a large number of organic elements that possess a certain degree of independence, and if these elements had a consciousness (and, of course, they have one to a certain degree), for them a complete person, of whose composition they are a part, in all likelihood would be only an abstraction. Each tiny nerve cell, each blood cell in your organism in all probability considers itself a genuine separate, individual entity, and it either knows nothing at all about you or you are for it only a general mass of entities foreign to it, like a collective, that is, metaphoric unit; and, it goes without saying, it is right for itself, just as you are right for yourself, too, if you consider humankind only a collection of separate people, if in humankind's unity you see only an empty abstraction. If we take an objective point of view, we must acknowledge that, just as the collective character of the human organism does not prevent a person from being a real, individual being, similarly the collective character of all of humankind does not prevent it from being just as real an individual entity. In this sense we recognize humankind as a genuine organic subject of historical development.

The component parts of every organism can be distinguished from the formative organic systems that are common to all its parts. Thus in the organism of a person the most important constitutive parts are the head, hands, chest, etc.; the most important organic systems common to the entire body are the nervous system, circulatory system, and muscular system. The elements of these systems are distributed through all the parts of the organism as essential for its life. In just the same way in the organism of hu-

---

a. This law, logically formulated by Hegel, was applied, from another point of view, to biology by Herbert Spencer. As far as I know, a consistent and complete application of it to the history of humankind has not been carried out.

mankind we distinguish, first, its component parts — tribes and peoples — and, second, certain formative systems and forms of existence common to humankind that belong to all humankind in all its parts as essential for its organic life. These parts constitute the *content proper* of historical development, and for this reason we must say a few words about them.

It goes without saying that the basic forms commonly accepted by human life must have their origin in principles that determine the very nature of a person. The nature of a person as such manifests itself in three basic forms of being: feeling, thinking, and active will;* each of these has two sides — exclusively personal and social. An isolated, purely subjective feeling; isolated thought or fantasy without any general, essential object; and spontaneous animal lust clearly cannot serve as formative principles or factors of commonly accepted human life as such. The significance of positive principles for this kind of life may consist of the following: only that feeling that strives to strengthen its existing condition by an objective expression of it, only that kind of thinking that strives for a specific objective content, only that will that has in mind definite general goals. In other words — feeling that has as its object *objective beauty*, thinking that has as its object *objective truth* (resultantly, thinking that comes to know, or knowledge), and will that has as its object *objective good*.

Of these three factors, the first spontaneous principle of social life is the will. As a formative principle of society, the will is determined by three primary relationships, or put another way, it manifests itself in three stages. For the achievement of any kind of objective good, it is first necessary to provide for the existence of its elementary subjects, i.e., of separate persons, which depends on their relationship to the natural world outside, on that activity a person directs toward this natural world in order to receive from it the means for existence. The social union that has this goal in mind and is based on the laborious, active cultivation of the natural world is an *economic society;* its primary elementary form is the family. The family, as comparative philology has demonstrated, has as its primary significance mainly an economic one, having as its basis an elementary division of labor.[b] This significance obtains in the family even today, although of

---

*Solovyov examines these "three basic forms of being" in the reverse order in which they are listed here.

b. See the evidence for this opinion in the first chapter of V. Miller's *Notes on Ariisk Mythology*.[2]

course it is complicated and sometimes almost completely eclipsed by the moral element.

The second basic form of society, which is inextricably linked with the first, determines the relationship of people not to the external natural world, but immediately to each other, and has as its direct object not people's labor, which is directed at nature, but people themselves in their interaction as members of a single collective whole. This is *political society*, or the *state* (πολιτεία, *res publica*). The task of economic society is the organization of *labor*, while the task of political society is the organization of *workers;* it goes without saying that the state has an economic side, just as economic society has a political side, and the distinction between them lies only in the fact that political interests have the predominating, central significance in the first while economic interests predominate in the second. Since there are *many* political societies, or states, along with the task of determining mutual relations among members of the state exists another task — of determining the relations among various states — international relations. But this second task and everything that derives from it is not an absolute necessity, since we must not negate the possibility of the realization of a universal state, to which the great monarchies of antiquity, especially the Roman Empire, came fairly close. The basic natural principle of a political society is *lawfulness*, or a *system of rights*, as an expression of fairness. Moreover, it goes without saying that the particular forms or manifestations of this principle, i.e., of *actual* laws and regulations in *actual* political societies, have a completely relative and temporary character, since they necessarily are determined by various changing historical conditions. Thus all actual judicial institutions that are measured by the criterion of the absolute principles of truth and good become abnormal, making the entire political existence of humankind appear as some kind of hereditary disease.

The third form of society is determined by the religious character of a person. A person desires not only *material* existence, which is provided by economic society, and not only *lawful* existence, which is given to him by political society, but he desires as well an *absolute* existence — one that is complete and eternal. Only the last of these is for him a genuine, supreme state of well-being, the summum bonum, with respect to which material goods attained through labor, and economic and formal goods attained through political activity, serve only as the means. Since the attainment of absolute existence, or eternal and blissful life, is the highest goal for everyone alike, this goal necessarily becomes the principle of social union, which may be called *spiritual* or *sacred society (the church)*.^c

Such are the three basic forms of social union, which derive from the essential will of a person or from his striving toward objective good. It is evident that the first form — economic society — has predominantly a material significance; the second — political society — manifests predominantly a formal character; and the third — spiritual society — must have a universal, or absolute, significance. The first represents the external basis, and the second the means, but only the third constitutes the goal. First and foremost, a person must live, and to this end material, economic labor is necessary in providing for his existence; he knows, however, that the fruits of this labor do not in themselves represent well-being for his essential will, and that his relations with other people that have in mind only the attainment of these material goods and that constitute economic society are not moral in and of themselves. To be moral, they must have the form of fairness or law, which is determined by political society, or the state. But the complete well-being of a person clearly does not depend on the *form* of his relations with other people, since even ideally fair activity does not yet produce bliss; if this bliss, in this manner, depends neither on what is gotten from the external world nor on the lawful and reasonable activity of the person himself, then clearly it is determined by those principles that are located outside the bounds of both the natural and the human worlds. Only that society that is based directly on relations with these transcendental principles can have as its direct objective the well-being of a person in his totality and absoluteness. This is what spiritual society or the church must be.

Let us now turn to the second sphere of universal human life — the sphere of knowledge. A person in his perceptual activity must bear in mind either the wealth of factual information obtained through the observation and experience of the external world and of human life, or the formal perfection of knowledge, its logical correctness as a system, or finally its universality, or absolute content. In other words, a person may bear in mind either material, existent truthfulness, or formal, logical truthfulness, or absolute truthfulness. The area of knowledge in which empirical content predominates and the main focus remains on material truthfulness is

---

c. These words refer only to the practical aspect of religion; the theoretical and creative aspects of it will be discussed in due course.

called *positive science;* knowledge determined mainly by general principles and that bears in mind predominantly logical perfection or formal truthfulness is called *abstract philosophy;* finally, knowledge that has absolute reality as its primary focus and point of departure is called *theology*. In positive science the center of everything is the real fact, in abstract philosophy it is the general idea, and in theology it is absolute being. Thus, the first provides the essential material basis for every type of knowledge, the second imparts an ideal form to it, and the third gives it absolute content and a universal goal. First and foremost, a person strives to know as much as possible about the world around him; subsequently, he realizes that material knowledge does not in and of itself constitute truth or, more precisely, that material truth in and of itself is not yet a genuine, complete truth. Material, factual knowledge, which depends on the evidence of the senses, is subject to the deception of the senses and can be an illusion; this form of knowledge does not manifest the attributes of its true nature — these attributes may be apprehended only in the domain of reason. But reason in its universal and essential propositions (logical and mathematical) has only a formal significance; it points out only the necessary conditions for the genuine attainment of knowledge, but does not provide its content. Moreover, as *our* reason, it may possess only a subjective significance *for us* as thinking beings. Thus if genuine, objective truth, constituting the goal of our knowledge, is not given in and of itself through external, observed reality, on which positive science depends and which however may turn out to be merely a sensory illusion — if, furthermore, it likewise is not given through pure reason, on which abstract philosophy is based and which may turn out to be merely subjective form — then it is clear that this genuine truth must be determined independently of external reality and of our reason by means of the absolute first principle of all of existence, which constitutes the subject of theology. Only this principle imparts genuine meaning and significance both to the concepts of philosophy and to the facts of science, without which the former become meaningless form and the latter undifferentiated matter.

It is not difficult to show the correspondence, or analogy, that exists among the separate fields or levels of the theoretical, perceptual sphere and similar levels of the practical or social sphere. Positive science and the economic field correspond in their common material character; abstract or pure rational philosophy corresponds in its formal character to political society, or the state; and theology in its absolute character corresponds to the spiritual or ecclesiastical field. This last correspondence — between theology and the church — is self-evident and there can be no doubt about it. Concerning the first two analogies, at first glance they seem too general and abstract. However, I shall point to two circumstances that provide factual support for these two analogies. First, it is indisputable that the idea of the state found its most zealous servants and defenders specifically in abstract philosophers; the closer the ideas of a thinker are to the category of pure rational philosophy, the greater the significance he attaches to the state. Thus the most extreme advocate of abstract philosophy in all its purity — Hegel — acknowledges the state as a complete, objective revelation or practical realization of an absolute idea. And in reality, in the social sphere only the state is founded on a formal, abstract, so to speak, leading principle — the principle of justice or law, which is none other than the practical expression of a logical foundation. The remaining two fields — the church and economic society — represent interests completely alien to abstract philosophy, namely, the church represents the interests of the heart while economic society — *sit venia verbo*[3] — represents the interests of the belly. On the other hand, the correspondence between positive science and economic society is underscored by a similar circumstance. Actually, the advocates of this view, which relates negatively both to the church and to formal statehood, want to connect all social relations to economics and consider economic interests the main, if not the sole, interest of society. The advocates of this view — socialists, at least the most consistent and sensible among them — are inclined in the theoretical sphere to attach exceptional importance to positive knowledge, reacting in a hostile manner toward theology and abstract philosophy,[d] while, in their turn, the extreme advocates of a positive scientific direction are inclined in the social sphere to give predominant importance to economic relations.

In turning our attention to the last basic sphere of human existence — the sphere of feelings — we must reiterate that feeling constitutes the subject of our consideration not from its subjective, personal side, but only insofar as it receives general, subjective expression, i.e., the beginning of creation. Material creation, for which the idea of beauty serves merely as an ornament in the context of utilitarian goals, I call *technical applied art*, the highest representative of which is architecture. Here the execution of cre-

---

d. Socialists-mystics and socialists-philosophers are separate exceptions; the entire mass of socialists is searching for a theoretical support only in positive science.

ative feeling[e] is aimed by a person directly at lowest [concerning levels of ascent from the material to the spiritual] external nature, and material is of essential significance. The kind of creation in which, on the contrary, the defining significance comes from aesthetic form — the form of beauty expressed in purely ideal images — is called *fine art (schöne Kunst, beaux arts)* and manifests itself in four forms: sculpture, painting, music, and poetry (it is easy to notice the gradual ascent from matter to spirit in these four forms of fine art). Sculpture is the most material art, the one closest to technical applied art in the highest sense of the latter — in architecture. Painting is already more ideal: there is no imitation of the corporeal in it, and bodies are depicted on a flat surface. Music possesses even more of a spiritual quality: it is no longer embodied in the material itself or on it, but rather in the movement and life of the substance — in sound. Finally, poetry (in the narrow sense of the term) finds its expression only in the spiritual element of the human word. Fine art has as its subject only the beautiful, but the beauty of artistic images does not yet constitute complete, total beauty; these images, ideally necessary in their form, have only an accidental, indefinite content — in simple terms, their subjects are accidental. In genuine, absolute beauty the content must be just as definite, necessary, and eternal as the form. But this type of beauty does not exist in our world: all the wonderful objects and phenomena in it are only accidental reflections of beauty itself, and not an organic part of it.

> And hungrily searching for it separately,
> We catch a reflection of eternal beauty;
> The forest rustles to us with the joyful news of it,
> Of it the stream resounds with a cold spray
> And the flowers, swaying, speak.
> And we love with a love that is fragmented:
> The quiet whisper of the pussy-willow by the stream,
> And the dear girl's face, bent over us,
> And the sparkling stars, and the beauty of the universe —
> Yet we're unable to connect these things with each other.[4]

---

e. "Creative feeling" may seem like a contradiction, but the fact of the matter is that a person, as a finite being, cannot be an absolute creator, i.e., cannot create out of his own self; therefore, his creation necessarily presupposes a perception of the highest creative powers in feeling.

Concerning the Law of Historical Development

Genuine, complete beauty may evidently be located only in the ideal world in and of itself, in the supernatural and superhuman world. The creative relationship of human feeling to this transcendental world is called *mysticism*.[f] Such a juxtaposition of mysticism with applied art may seem unexpected and paradoxical, since the relationship of mysticism to creation is unclear. To be sure, no one would have any difficulty acknowledging that mysticism and applied art have the following traits in common: (1) both have as their basis feeling (not perception and not active will); (2) both have as their weapon or means imagination or fantasy (not reflection and not external activity); (3) both presuppose in their subject ecstatic inspiration (not calm consciousness). Nevertheless, for the uninitiated it remains doubtful that mysticism and applied art can be simply different manifestations or aspects of one and the same primary factor — doubtful because an exclusively subjective meaning is usually ascribed to mysticism; in mysticism is negated the capacity for the kind of definition and objective expression and realization that undoubtedly are a part of applied art. But this is an error that comes from the fact that no one has the slightest idea of what is properly assumed under the term "mysticism," so that for most people this term has become a synonym for everything that is unclear and incomprehensible — which is completely natural. This is due to the fact that, although the sphere of mysticism possesses an absolute clarity by itself, and it alone can clarify everything else, precisely as a result of this its light is unbearable for weak and unprotected eyes, and it plunges them into absolute darkness. A further explanation of the objectively creative aspect of mysticism would force me to touch upon the kinds of things that I feel are premature to discuss. Concerning its relationship to other levels of existence, it is clear that mysticism occupies in the sphere of creation the same place as theology and spiritual society in their respective spheres, in exactly the same way as fine art in its predominantly formal character presents an analogy with philosophy and political society, and technical applied art obviously corresponds to positive science and economic society.

 f. It is necessary to make a strict distinction between two kinds of mysticism [*mistika* and *mistitsizm* — trans.]: the first is the direct, spontaneous relationship of our spirit to the transcendental world, while the second refers to the reflection of our mind concerning the relationship and forms of the particular current of philosophy that will be discussed below. *Mistika* and *mistitsizm* relate to each other in a way similar to *èmpiriia* and *èmpirizm* [empiricism — trans.].

GENERAL HISTORICAL INTRODUCTION

We have examined the basic forms of the organism common to humankind. The following table presents them synoptically:

	I Sphere of Creation	II Sphere of Knowledge	III Sphere of Practical Activity
Subjective basis	feeling	thinking	will
Objective principle	beauty	truth	common good
1st level: absolute	Mysticism	Theology	Spiritual society (church)
2nd level: formal	Fine art	Abstract philosophy	Political society (the state)
3rd level: material	Technical applied art	Positive science	Economic society (the *zemstvo*)

It is worth noting that among the three general spheres, preeminent significance belongs to the sphere of creation, and since in this same sphere the most important place is occupied by mysticism, this latter possesses the significance of the genuine, supreme origin of the entire life of the universal human organism, which is understandable, since in mysticism this life is located in a direct, intimate link with the reality of the absolute first principle, with divine life. With special pleasure I can point out here that the great importance of mysticism is understood in modern times by two philosophers of the most freethinking and even rather negative views, philosophers who are hostile to every type of positive religion and whom, in the light of this, it is impossible in any way to suspect of possessing a traditional partiality to this question. I have in mind the famous Schopenhauer and the most recent continuer of his ideas — Hartmann. The first sees in mysticism and the asceticism based on it the origin of spiritual rebirth for a person, which reveals for him a higher moral life and "a better consciousness" *(das bessere Bewusstsein):* only in this life does a person actually liberate himself from blind, animal desire and the evil and suffering linked with it. For Hartmann mysticism is the fundamental beginning of everything essential and exalted in personal and universal human life.

According to the law of development, the universal human organism must pass through three stages (three phases, three moments of its development) that relate to the cited spheres and levels of its existence. In the first stage these levels exist in an undifferentiated or merged form, and thus each of them does not possess actual, separate existence independently, but instead exists only potentially. This undifferentiation, as noted above, cannot be absolute, since in such a case there would not be any kind of organization, not even in embryonic form. It consists of a higher, or absolute level, which engulfs and hides in itself all the rest, not allowing them any independent manifestation. In the second stage the lower levels come to life from out of the control of the higher one and seek unconditional freedom; first, they rebel together, undifferentiatedly against the higher origin, and reject it, but for each of them to attain complete development this lower level must affirm itself exclusively not only with respect to the higher one but also concerning all the others. It must similarly reject them as well, so that in the wake of the general struggle of the lower elements against the higher one necessarily comes an internecine war in the sphere of the lower ones themselves. And in the meantime the highest level itself, as a result of this process, separates itself and defines itself as such, gains its freedom, and thus causes the possibility of a new unity. This is because, on the one hand, none of the lower levels can achieve exclusive domination (which would be fatal for humankind), and therefore, for their unity they must seek a certain higher center outside themselves — this function can be satisfied only by an absolute level. On the other hand, the latter no longer requires their external subordination or absorption, such as was the case during the first stage, because, as a consequence of the preceding detachment or isolation, it gained its own independent existence and may serve for the lower levels as the origin of a free unity, which is necessary for them. Thus the altered condition of the levels as a consequence of the process of their isolation leads finally to a new, completely organic combination based on the free, conscious subordination of lower levels to a higher one as the necessary center of their own life. The realization of this new unity forms the third stage of common [human] development. Let us now examine these stages in their historical reality.

There is no doubt that the first, most ancient period of human history bears as its most dominant characteristic a merging, or undifferentiation, of all spheres and levels of universal life. There is no doubt that originally a clear distinction did not exist among spiritual, political, and economic societies; the first forms of economic union — the family and the clan — also possessed a political and religious significance, being the first government and the first church. Similarly undifferentiated were theology, philosophy and science, mysticism, and fine and technical art. The representatives of spiritual power — the high priests — were also the rulers and guardians of society; they were the theologians, philosophers, and scientists. Being situated in direct mystical contact with the higher powers of existence, they also, in the light of the goals of this contact, directed artistic and technical activity. The most ancient temples were not only buildings designated for a social cult and combining for this purpose technical skills and fine art — they were also mysterious sanctuaries where the highest potentials were visually and palpably made manifest. Everything in these temples was directed toward the goal of facilitating these manifestations. It is common knowledge that the various forms of art in the most ancient period were distinguished, first, by being much more closely linked with each other than is the case today — they had not yet completely revealed their characteristics, so that it was impossible to separate ancient poetry from music, ancient painting from sculpture or even architecture (for example, on Egyptian monuments); and second, by the fact that they all served a single hierarchical goal, i.e., they were subordinated by and even merged with mysticism. The absolute level, the formal and material level, and subsequently the spheres of creative work, knowledge, and practical activity were assembled here in one focus. As a matter of fact, during this epoch in the area of knowledge there existed no distinction at all among theology, philosophy, and science — this entire area represented a single interconnected whole, which may be called *theosophy;* the area of the church, government, and economic society initially emerged as the same kind of unity in the form of a *theocracy;* finally, mysticism, fine art, and technical art were akin to a single mystical creative process, or *theurgy,*[g] while all these areas together formed a single religious whole. It goes without saying that in the historical development of the ancient world this interconnectedness was more or less total and the

---

g. One should not assume that a theocracy existed only where there was a dominion of high priests as a caste: A civil government was also a theocracy, since it was based on religion; the *res publica* was characterized by a sacred quality *(sacer populus romanus);* it constituted both a church and a government — i.e., as a matter of fact, it was neither the one nor the other in the modern sense of each word, but rather manifested their undifferentiatedness. The rulers and military leaders made sacrifices to the gods and were thus of a religious bent; on the other hand, the highest priest was also the *rex,* and originally not in name only *(rex sacrorum),*[5] but in reality as well.

force of this original unity was not preserved to the same degree at all times and in every part of the ancient world; very early in Greece and Rome (and in part even in India) one may already note the beginnings of a progressive separation of the various spheres and elements of human existence. Nevertheless, it must be acknowledged that in the universal consciousness of humankind the original interconnectedness was shaken decisively and to its very foundations only with the advent of Christianity, when for the first time the *sacrum* was separated from the *profanum*.[6] In this respect, as a force that dealt the final blow to this external, involuntary unity, Christianity represented the beginning of genuine freedom. Let us trace this decisive detachment and isolation of the spheres and levels that originated with the advent of Christianity, first in the most external and therefore the most definitive sphere — practical activity and the forms of society based on it.

First, according to the law of development, the two lowest levels separate *together* from the highest one as the *profanum* or *naturale* separates from the *sacrum* or *divinum*. More precisely, the second level, which still includes the third, separates from the first: the government, still merged with economic society, separates from the church. This separation occurs necessarily by the nature of things, according to the logic of the facts, independently of the conscious, personal will of the people. Christianity, as it manifested itself in the consciousness of its first proponents, did not at all strive for any kind of social upheaval: its entire task consisted of the religio-moral rebirth of individual people in light of the approaching end of the world. The proponents of Christianity did not at all view government power with hostility, since they perceived themselves as children of God, as opposed to the pagan world — the kingdom of evil and the devil ("we know that we are of God, while the whole world lies in a state of evil"). They saw in government the unintentional instrument of God, intended for the containment and control of the dark forces of paganism. As a spiritual society, Christianity opposed itself to the other, carnal society — paganism — not the government as such. But herein precisely lies the separation of the church from the state. In reality, once the Christian church designated itself as the only spiritual, sacred society, considering everything else to be *profanum*, by this very act it took away the government's entire previous significance — it repudiated the sacred republic. In recognizing the government solely as a restraining, repressive force, Christians stripped it of any positive spiritual content. For them the emperor — the last god of the pagan world — could be only the chief administrator of the police. This relationship negated the very principle of ancient society, which entailed specifically the deification of the republic and the emperor as its representative, the merging of spiritual and secular principles. Hence the emperors, in persecuting the Christians, were acting not as bearers of governmental powers in the narrow sense of the term (Christianity was not threatening this power at all), but as bearers of the entire ancient consciousness.

For the original Christians the universe was divided into two kingdoms — the kingdom of God, which consisted of them, and the kingdom of evil origins, consisting of stubborn pagans to whom governmental powers also belonged, since it [the government] identified itself with the pagan world. This view was developed in detail, as is well known, by Augustine in his *De civitate Dei*.[7] But this was only the latest, belated expression of an earlier point of view. This view in actuality could not be preserved when the representative of paganism — governmental power in the person of Constantine the Great — not only ceased his enmity toward Christianity, but also stood directly beneath its banner; subsequently when the entire pagan world, at least externally, became Christian, the church sanctioned the transformed government and united with it, though only mechanically. An external compromise took place. The church was linked with the government, but it could not internally penetrate it, assimilate it, and make it an organ of itself, because early Christianity itself no longer had (or, better, did not yet have) enough internal strength to achieve this goal. The initial days of miraculous, supernatural excitement, the days of the apostles and the martyrs, had passed, while the time of a conscious moral rebirth had not yet arrived.

The Roman-Byzantine government retained a completely pagan character — not a single substantive change took place in it. It is impossible to identify a single, minimally significant distinction between the governmental structure of the pagan Diocletian and the quasi-Christian Theodosius I or Justinian: one notes the same principle, the same institutions. The principle is Roman, with pagan laws, while the institutions are a combination of Roman republican forms and Eastern despotism. Justinian, who convened the ecumenical council, for which Origen was not orthodox enough — this same Justinian published the systematic code of Roman laws for his Christian empire. Meanwhile Christianity had appeared precisely with the goal of abolishing the power of the law. Christianity distinguishes itself as a kingdom of grace, and for it the law is an instrument of God only in the Old Testament out of the hard-heartedness of the Israelites and also, as noted above, in the pagan world as a repressive force that controls the offspring of the devil but has no significance for the children of God or for the church. If at this time, when the kingdom of the devil had evidently disappeared, when all the members of the government had also become members of the church and concomitantly God's children, the external law still retained its power, then this obviously proved that the transformation was only nominal. To be sure, it would be childish to lay the blame for this on the church: the crux of the matter was that the transformational power of Christianity could not spread at once throughout the entire organism of humankind as long as this organism had not yet completed its own necessary development, had not yet attained in full measure the spiritual maturity of Christ.

Thus, since the time of Constantine the Great we have the coexistence of two heterogeneous social forms, the church and the state, which differ from each other in their basic character and their basic principle. In the East the state, due to its old, tight organization, turned out to be stronger than the church and de facto subordinated the church to itself, but precisely because this organization was exclusively traditional, deprived of any new internal bases, the state at this point could not develop — it fell along with the Eastern Church to Islam. A different relationship obtains, as is well known, in the West. Here, on the one hand, because the church was obliged to deal not with the organized Byzantine government but rather with the disorderly hordes of Germanic barbarians, it acquired enormous power; on the other hand, these same Germanic barbarians who externally accepted Catholicism and subordinated themselves to it, but retained their internal distinctiveness, contributed to history new principles of life (corresponding to the second stage of universal human development) — the consciousness of absolute freedom, the supreme significance of the individual. Opposed to the chaotic world of the Germanic conquerors, the church naturally had to appropriate for itself the tradition of Roman unity, and had to become either the Roman Caesarean church or an ecclesiastical state, which necessarily provoked hostility from the secular Germanic state as an illegal invasion of its sphere of influence. In this manner, in the West the church and state existed as hostile forces battling each other. But something larger than this appeared: in the Middle Ages in the West we note for the first time a clear separation of political society and economic society

— of the state and the district councils.* The external reason for this separation was the circumstance that the Germanic princes' armed forces, constituting the governmental structure of the Middle Ages, dominated an entire social stratum of Celts-Slavs, whom they had dominated and enslaved. These peoples, deprived of all their political rights, were solely of an economic significance, as a labor force; however, because they were Christians, they could not be absolutely excluded from the social structure, as had slaves in antiquity. Thus they constituted a social stratum, a particular society — an economic society or a district council, equally foreign to the Roman Church and to the Germanic state. Soon this lower stratum began to develop its own religion — Catharism or Albigensianism, which first appeared in the Slavic East under the name of Bogomilism,† and from there spread throughout the Celtic-Slavic world. This religion, however, perished in rivers of blood, having aroused in equal measure the hostility of the Roman Church (which at that time was at the height of its powers) and the feudal government.

The crusade against the Albigensians constituted the last major act of the common allied activity of the Roman Church and the feudal government.[8] The division between them, which took place in Germany earlier, soon spread throughout the greater part of Europe. At the beginning of the Middle Ages, after the short-lived empire of Charlemagne, secular society, broken up into a multitude of regions and having in reality as many heads as there were mighty feudal lords, was extremely weak; the only common unifying force in the West was the Roman Church, which was attempting to amass political power for itself. To fight this force successfully, secular society had to attain a solid unity and defeat the feudal lords who were hostile to it. Only national kings could accomplish this task, since as a result of the significant isolation of separate nationalities the Holy Germanic-Roman Empire remained as merely the shadow of a great name. This is not the place to describe how the process of political unification

---

zemstvo (Russ.) — an elective district council in prerevolutionary Russia.

†The religious movement called Bogomilism emerged in the twelfth and the thirteenth centuries. Similar to some of the early Christian heretics, the Bogomils (friends of God) believed in two Gods: the good God who created heaven, and the evil God who created the world and the Jewish religion of the Old Testament. The Bogomils accepted the New Testament but rejected the miracles of Christ. They were considered heretics and eventually disappeared as a group. See *The Orthodox Church: A Well-Kept Secret*, by Fr. George Nicozisin, a religious pamphlet used by the Greek Orthodox Archdiocese of North America, p. 87.

was achieved in Europe; it is enough to say that by the end of the Middle Ages both the Roman Church and feudalism had been equally shaken up, while the real force was the political power manifested by the national kings.

The Roman Church, itself having become a state after it captured a political region, could not coexist with the new, more powerful political system; and since the government could not yet separate itself completely from every church (because religious beliefs still retained their strength and significance for the people's consciousness), it had to acknowledge the pressing need for a new, altered church. A church reform was required, one that would oppose to the Roman ecclesiastical state a state church, i.e., a church subordinated to the state and defined by the latter in its practical relations. Protestantism completely answered this requirement. If the heresies of the Middle Ages revealed the attempts to create a district council–style Celto-Slavic church, Protestantism without a doubt gave rise to a state and Germanic church. Herein lies its success predominantly in the Germanic lands. But it goes without saying that this success was also reflected throughout the rest of Europe in the mutual relations between the church and the state; whether sooner or later, these relations had to change everywhere in the Protestant sense.[h]

The beginning of the new era* was thus characterized in the social sphere by a decisive isolation of the government and formation of a new state church. But the government, as a purely formal entity, could not increase its strength by itself, without depending on some real force. Indeed, from the very beginning of its struggle against feudalism and the church, the state sought the help of the district council, which was represented by the so-called *tiers-état*,[9] which in this way received some degree of political significance. However, the link between the state and the district council was purely external and transient; they were united only against common enemies. When these enemies were defeated, the monarchical power (in confirmation of the general principle of Western development) began to strive for complete independence, began to attach to itself absolute significance in its exclusive centralization; instead of serving the peo-

---

h. It goes without saying that this does not exhaust the significance of Protestantism, which was not only a church but also a general religious reform.

*Solovyov has in mind the Age of Enlightenment (the latter half of the seventeenth century and the eighteenth century).

ple's interests, it became a hostile force that oppressed and exploited the people. But in adopting this behavior, monarchical absolutism deprived itself of any real foundation, and the moment of its greatest triumph was the beginning of its downfall. In its struggle against the church and feudalism, state power depended not on some higher principle but rather solely on actual force — this force, however, belonged not to the government per se, but was provided by the district council, and the monarchical power thus possessed real significance as the representative of the people.[i] When governmental absolutism refused this role and separated from the people in its exclusive self-affirmation, it became necessary for the real force on which it had formerly depended to turn against it. It became necessary for the district council to revolt against absolute government and transform it into an undifferentiated form, into the executive instrument of popular voting. This transformation, constituting the main result of the French Revolution, spread in one form or another throughout the Western continent (in England it was achieved earlier by a more gradual and complex process). Europe was defeated by revolutionary France, and only with the help of an outside power — Russia — was it able to free itself from external submission to it; internally Europe remained infused with the revolutionary principle, and soon everywhere in the place of absolute monarchy there appeared a new governmental form: constitutional, or parliamentary. But from the time of the French Revolution, which seemingly by a single blow shattered the appeal of the old, traditional foundations, the negative course of history proceeded with extraordinary speed. The governmental forms that emerged from the Revolution had scarcely begun to spread throughout Europe when the clear realization emerged that this was only a transition, that it was not the main thing.

The populace or the district council, having revolted in the West against an absolute church and absolute state, and having defeated them in its revolutionary movement, by itself could not maintain its unity and safety. It broke apart into classes hostile to one another, and subsequently also necessarily had to break apart into individuals hostile to each other. The social organism of the West, having separated at first into particular organisms that excluded each other, finally had to break up into its last ele-

---

i. A normal relationship obtains when the government does not serve the people and the people do not serve the government, but both equally serve the same higher principle.

ments, into the atoms of society, i.e., into separate individuals; corporate, caste egotism was transformed into personal egotism. The Revolution transferred supreme power to the people; in place of the feudal principle of lineage, in place of the politico-theological principle of absolute monarchy by God's grace, it established the principle of sovereignty of the people. But the term "the people" must be understood here as the simple sum of separate individuals, the entire unity of which consists of the fortuitous convergence of desires and interests — a convergence that could just as well not exist. Having destroyed those traditional connections, those ideal foundations that in old Europe made each separate individual only an element of a higher social group and, in separating humanity, united persons — having destroyed these connections, the revolutionary movement left each individual to himself and concomitantly destroyed his organic distinction from the others. In old Europe this distinction, and consequently the inequality of individuals, was conditioned by their belonging to one or another social group and by the place they occupied in that group. With the destruction of these groups in their former significance this ideal inequality also disappeared; what remained was only a lower, natural inequality of personal forces. From the voluntary manifestation of these forces new forms of life should have developed in the place of the shattered world. But the revolutionary movement did not provide any positive grounds for such new creative activity. It is easy to see in reality that the principle of freedom, taken by itself, has only a negative connotation. I can live and act freely, i.e., without encountering any arbitrary obstacles or constraints, but this obviously in no way defines the positive purpose of my activity, the content of my life. In old Europe human life received its ideal content from the Catholic faith, on the one hand, and from knightly feudalism on the other. This ideal content gave old Europe its relative unity and lofty heroic strength, although already concealed in this content was the beginning of that dualism that necessarily had to lead to the resulting disintegration. The Revolution ultimately rejected the old ideals, which was of course necessary, but because of its negative character it could not provide new ones; it liberated individual elements, gave them an absolute significance, but deprived their activity of its essential foundation and nourishment.

For this reason we see that the excessive development of individualism in the contemporary West leads directly to its opposite — a universal depersonalization and vulgarization. The extreme preoccupation with self-identity, in not finding an appropriate subject for itself, is transformed into an empty and petty egotism that reduces everyone to the same level. The only substantive distinction and inequality that still exists among people in the West is that between the wealthy and the proletariat; the only greatness, the only supreme body that retains actual power there is the mighty force and power of capital. The Revolution, which affirmed the principle of democracy, in reality to date has produced only a plutocracy. The people govern themselves *de jure;* but they are *de facto*[10] governed by a very small minority — the wealthy bourgeoisie, the capitalists. Since a plutocracy by its very nature is accessible to everyone alike, it remains a kingdom of free enterprise, or competition. But this freedom and equality of rights are far from being the direct result of the unconditional existence of inherited property, and its concentration in the hands of a small minority creates in the bourgeoisie a separate, privileged class; the overwhelming majority of members of the working class, deprived of all property despite its abstract freedom and equality of rights, in reality becomes an enslaved class of proletarians. However, the existence of the perpetual proletarian class, which constitutes the dominant trait of today's West, is precisely in this regard denied any kind of justification. This is because if the old order depended on well-known, absolute principles, the contemporary plutocracy may in its own interest rely on the strength of the fact, on historical conditions. But these conditions change; historical conditions also created ancient slavery, which did not prevent it from disappearing. If we speak about fairness, as soon as it is acknowledged that power derives from material wealth (since the latter is considered the highest goal of life), is it not fair for the wealth and the power linked with it to belong to those who produce it, i.e., the workers? It goes without saying that capital, i.e., the result of previous labor, is just as necessary for the production of wealth as genuine labor, but no one has ever proved the necessity of their absolute separation, i.e., that one person must be *only* a capitalist while others must be *only* workers. Thus emerges the aspiration of labor, i.e., the workers, to take possession of the capital, which constitutes the most pressing task of *socialism.* But the latter also has a more general significance: the final, categorical detachment and self-affirmation of economic society, as opposed to political society and spiritual society. Contemporary socialism demands that social forms be determined solely on the basis of economic relationships in order for governmental power to be only an organ of the economic interests of the

Concerning the Law of Historical Development

majority of the people. Concerning spiritual society, it of course completely rejects contemporary socialism.[j]

Such was the last word of social development during the second stage of human history, as represented by Western civilization. This second stage was characterized in the social sphere, as we have seen, first by the separation of secular society in general from ecclesiastical society, and then by the disintegration of secular society itself into the government and the district council, so that in fact three societal organizations emerged, each of which in its turn utilized the higher levels of government, trying to exclude or subordinate to itself the two remaining organizations. This process was completely continuous and necessary, and today the approaching supremacy in the West of the third societal organization — the economic, in its principles supported by socialism — represents the same kind of necessary step on the road of Western development that was made in its time by the supremacy of the Catholic Church, and subsequently by the absolutism of government. But it is evident that the necessity of all three of these exclusive supremacies is solely historic, and hence conditional and temporary; if no reasonable and dispassionate person can believe in the absolute necessity for humankind of the Catholic Church or the monarchy à la Louis XIV, it would be just as silly to see in socialism the final universal revelation that must regenerate humanity. In reality, no alteration of social relations, and no re-creation of social forms, can satisfy those eternal needs and questions that in fact define human life. If we assume even the total realization of socialism's aims, when all people will utilize equally the benefits and comforts of civilized life, then these eternal questions about the inner content of life and the higher purpose of human activity will rise before us with even greater force and persistence. The answer to all these questions obviously cannot be found in the area of practical relations; to find it, we must necessarily delve into the sphere of knowledge. And in this regard, what does Western civilization offer us?

A characteristic trait of Western development and the sphere of knowledge is the progressive separation and exclusive independence of its

---

j. Old socialism (of the first half of the current century) in some of its schools tried to merge spiritual society with economic, i.e., in fact, attributing to the latter the significance of the former, making a church out of a workers' union — a ridiculous endeavor that produced only comical results.

three levels. Initially a division took place between sacred knowledge, or theology, and secular, or natural, knowledge. In the latter during the Middle Ages the distinction had not yet developed between philosophy proper and empirical science — both together constituted a single philosophy that was acknowledged as the handmaiden of theology, and only toward the end of the Middle Ages (during the epoch of the Renaissance) was philosophy freed of this subservient position. The circumstances of this liberation are described in the words that follow. First, theology, in relying on the authority of the church because of the natural affinity between the two, for this very reason was deprived of its strength by the practical liberation of people from ecclesiastical power. Subsequently, theology in its aspiration for exclusive supremacy in the sphere of knowledge carried out unlawful seizures in the areas of philosophy and science. It specifically sought by means belonging only to it, i.e., presupposing the authority of the Scriptures and the church, to affirm certain positions, which in their essence were subject only to the authority of reason or experience, it being the case naturally that such positions at that time had been accepted precisely in a connotation opposed to reason and experience.

Meanwhile, this very scholasticism by its formal structures facilitated the development of philosophical thought, which during the epoch of the Renaissance was strengthened by an even better acquaintance with Greek philosophy. When these horizons were further expanded, the contradiction became sharply delineated, and theological authority decisively began to waver. Finally, in its internal development scholastic theology, like everything that is one-sided and is moving toward its opposite, was leading to the acknowledgment of the exclusive rights of reason, to rationalism, which, starting from the sixteenth century, had already become the dominant mode of thought.[k]

During the Renaissance, philosophy, along with what was still inseparable from it — the science concealed, so to speak, in it — struggled in the capacity of natural knowledge against theology as supernatural knowledge (and in scholasticism often antinatural as well), and soon defeated it. In the seventeenth century scholastic theology already belonged to history, although its stillborn products, and also its attempts to regain its former sig-

---

[k]. The dialectical necessity of a transition from the supremacy of authority to that of reason is noted by me in my work "The Crisis of Western Philosophy," at the beginning of the introduction.

nificance, appear to this day.¹ However, after the victory of natural science a division emerged in natural science itself. Already at the beginning of the modern era there appeared two mutually opposed intellectual currents — the rationalist and the empirical; the latter developed in the eighteenth century, while in the nineteenth century it even more decisively joined the positive sciences, which had separated from philosophy, and entered into battle with the rationalist, or purely philosophical, current. This was justified by the fact that at the end of the last [eighteenth] and beginning of the current century rationalist philosophy, having finally in the critique of pure reason freed itself from any ties with theology, began to strive for exclusive supremacy in the area of knowledge and affirmed itself in Hegelianism as absolute knowledge. Hegel possessed the same significance for philosophy as Ludwig XIV for government, and just as Ludwig XIV by his absolutism forevermore compromised the meaning of monarchical government in the West, so the absolutism of Hegel led to the final downfall of rationalist philosophy. At this point there emerged a *tiers-état* — positive science, which nowadays in its turn expresses its claims on absolute supremacy in the area of knowledge, and likewise wants to be all-important. This claim is decisively exhibited by what is called "positivism," which attempts to unite all the separate sciences into a single general system that must represent the entire aggregate of human knowledge. According to this view, theology and philosophy (which here take on the generic term "metaphysics") are outdated, though in their own time necessary, fictions. But positivism goes even further. Similar to how socialism not only negates the significance of the church and the state and wants to transfer all their power to the district council or economic society, but yet in this very same society strives to destroy the distinction between the capitalists and the workers in favor of the latter — analogous to this, positivism, too, not only negates theology and philosophy, attributing exclusive knowledge to positive science, but also in this very science wants to destroy the distinction between the cognition of causes and the cognition of phenomena as such, emphasizing exclusively this last type of cognition. In general, positivism in the area of knowledge completely corresponds with socialism in the social sphere and likewise manifests in its own sphere the necessary final word of Western development; for this reason every ad-

---

1. As, for example, in the works of Abbott Gratry, in Shtyokl's history of the philosophy of the Middle Ages, etc.¹¹

mirer of Western civilization must consider himself a positivist if he wants to be consistent.

However, when we examine the absolutism of empirical science, which was heralded by positivism, from the universal human, not a limited Western, point of view, we easily see its insignificance. Just as socialism, even if all its utopias were to be realized, could not in any way satisfy the essential needs of the human will — needs for moral peacefulness and bliss[m] — precisely so positivism, even if its *pia desideria*[13] were to be fulfilled and all its phenomena, even the most complicated, were reduced to simple and general laws, could not in any way satisfy the higher demands of the human *mind*, which seeks not factual knowledge (i.e., the ascertainment) of phenomena and their general laws, but rather the reasonable explanation of them. Science as positivism understands it — having refused to consider the questions *why* and *for what reason* and *what is*, leaving for itself only the uninteresting question *what exists* or *what appears* — by this very position acknowledges its theoretical groundlessness and concomitantly its inability to elaborate the higher content of human life and activity.[n]

The same result was arrived at by Western development in the area of creative work. Contemporary Western art cannot capture the ideal content of life for the simple reason that it itself has lost it. In the sphere of creative work we see in the West the same alteration in the three supremacies. In the Middle Ages unfettered art does not exist; everything is subordinated to mysticism. Since the epoch of the Renaissance, as a result of the general weakening of religious principles, on the one hand, and of the special influence of classical art that was once again discovered, on the other hand, the fine art of form emerges, first in painting (and sculpture), then in poetry, and finally in music. In our century a third supremacy developed — that of technical art, which is purely practical and utilitarian. Art for art's sake, i.e., for the sake of beauty, is as foreign to our century as is mystical creative

---

m. Already for the reason that real bliss presupposes eternity:
   Know that for love and happiness I need eternal life,
   Happiness asks for eternity, life demands eternity . . .
   This oppressive thought weighs upon the soul,
   The heart gnaws like a snake, and poisons bliss.[12]

n. Because to achieve this end it would be necessary to answer the question, "*What should exist?*" Empirical science only knows what exists, but the first evidently does not follow from the second, the ideal does not follow from reality, the goal does not result from the fact.

work; if purely artistic works still appear, then it is only in the form of amusing trifles. The imitation of superficial reality and a narrow little utilitarian idea — a so-called current — are all that is required nowadays of an artistic work. Art has been transformed into a trade — everyone knows this. It goes without saying that exclusively religious and likewise exclusively formal art are both one-sided and hence had to lose their significance, but contemporary realism, being no less one-sided than the others, in addition is deprived of the depth of the first and the ideal refinement of the second — its only merits are its lightness and general accessibility.

Thus economic socialism in the social sphere, positivism in the epistemological sphere, and utilitarian realism in the artistic sphere — this constitutes the final word of Western civilization. Is this then also the final word of all human development? The immutable laws of this development answer in the negative. Western civilization by its general character represents only the second, transitional phase in the organic process of humankind, but for the completeness of this process a third is necessary. Moreover, it should not be forgotten that as a result of the negative and vulgar character of the final results at which Western civilization has arrived, these results could not become general or universal, could not internally, radically cancel out the old, relatively higher principles that were displaced by them only because of the consciousness of a superficial majority. In this way all political (and, in the future, social as well) revolutions may destroy any historical forms of government whatsoever, but government's most formal principle is inaccessible to them. On the other hand, government could defeat, but could not destroy, its old opponent — the church: this old enemy still stands over it, at a time when government for a long time has been struggling with new enemies. Philosophy is considered outdated, but both it and theology have preserved their adherents from among the best minds. Furthermore, mysticism not only continues to exist in secret, but from time to time shows itself in reality as well (even if only in the background), producing a comical panic among sober minds. Ideal art has also not died, and not without a reverberation does the poet's voice ring out:

> The truth is still the same! Through the rainy gloom
> Believe in the sacred star of inspiration,
> In the name of beauty row together
> Against the current.

> Friends, row on! In vain do the abusers
> Ridicule us by their arrogance —
> Soon we, the conquerors of the waves,
> Will reach the shore victoriously with our sacred treasures.[14]

Such inner vitality of allegedly outdated forms is completely understandable: the final results of Western civilization in their narrowness and shallowness can satisfy only the corresponding narrow and shallow minds and hearts. As long as religious sensibility and philosophical inquiry exist in humankind, as long as humankind retains its aspiration for the eternal and ideal, mysticism, pure art, theology, metaphysics, and the church will remain undefeatable, notwithstanding all the successes and claims of the lower levels [of vulgar artistic currents], whose champions are only a mental and moral *vulgus*.[15] These lower levels cannot replace the higher ones with themselves, for the same reason that the satisfaction of bestial needs cannot replace the satisfaction of spiritual needs and the vulgar Aphrodite cannot possess the wreath of the heavenly Aphrodite. To be sure, those forms in which the heavenly Aphrodite appeared in the West could only be exceptional ones and, consequently, imperfect, which made their relative decline unavoidable; in truth, however, these forms can evidently be abolished internally only by the best, i.e., most complete, fullest realization of those same higher principles, and not at all by the negative action of lower principles. It is evident that in reality, as soon as, for example, religious impulses arise in a person, a bad religion can in truth be abolished only by a better one, and in no way by simple atheism. The same holds true for the existence of metaphysical necessity: a bad metaphysics can be abolished by a good metaphysics, and not by the simple negation of all metaphysics.

But let us go further. Not only is it impossible for separate low levels at the second stage of development to attain the exclusive predominance for which they strive, but also this entire second stage, or phase, of historical development manifested by Western civilization cannot displace from history the representatives of its first phase — a phase of substantial unity and undifferentiation. In reality, Western civilization did not become universal, but turned out to be defenseless against an entire culture — the Islamic East. In historical Western Christianity, as soon as those features that constituted its one-sidedness were delineated, as soon as it became obvious that this Christian world in its exclusivity was striving only to manifest the stage of disintegration and struggle in historical development, the forces of the ancient East, at first completely paralyzed by Christianity, once again came alive in the form of Islam, which not only did not capitulate to the Christian West, but indeed successfully mounted a campaign against it. To this day Europe, with all its development, has had to endure and acknowledge on its territory its age-old enemy, and finally even enter into an alliance with it. And this was necessary, because the second stage, taken separately and examined not as a transition to the third, but for itself, not only is not higher, but in a certain sense is even lower than the first.

We saw in actuality that both in the sphere of social relations and in the sphere of knowledge and creative work a second force,º which directed the development of Western civilization, being itself predisposed to this, irrepressibly led to a general decomposition into lower component parts, and to a loss of any universal content and all absolute principles of existence. And if the Eastern world, representing the first stage — of exclusive monism — destroyed a person's independence and affirmed only a non-human god, Western civilization strove first and foremost for the exclusive affirmation of a godless person, i.e., a person taken in his external superficial separateness and reality, and in this false position acknowledged simultaneously both as the only deity and as an insignificant atom: as a deity for himself, subjectively, and as an insignificant atom, objectively, with respect to the external world, of which he is a separate particle in the endless expanse and a transient phenomenon in endless time. Understandably, everything that such a person could produce would be fractional, particular, deprived of internal unity and absolute content, and limited solely to superficiality, without ever achieving a genuine focus.

A separate egotistical interest, accidental fact, minor detail — atomism in life, atomism in science, and atomism in art — this is the last word of Western civilization. And to the extent that exclusive monism is higher than this atomism, to the extent that even a bad beginning is better than complete anarchy or headlessness, to this extent the first stage of development is higher than the second, taken separately, and the Islamic East is higher than Western civilization. This civilization elaborated particular forms and the external material of life, but did not give humankind the inner content of

---

o. I use the word "force" here to indicate the general principle that defines a certain stage in the historical development of humankind, leaving aside the question of what inherently constitutes this force.

this very life. Having isolated separate elements, it took them to the most extreme degree of development that was possible only in their separateness, but without an organic connection they were deprived of a living spirit, and all this wealth became dead stock. And if the history of humankind is not meant to end with this negative result, this insignificance, if a new historic force is supposed to emerge, its task will no longer consist of elaborating the separate elements of life and knowledge, and of creating new cultural forms. Rather, its task will consist of revitalizing and spiritualizing the elements that are hostile and lifeless in their hostility to each other by means of higher conciliatory principles, and of giving them a common, absolute content, by which they will be freed of exclusive self-affirmation and mutual negation. But where can this absolute content of life and knowledge be found? It cannot be located in a person himself as a particular, relative being; it cannot be contained in the external world, either, which manifests only the lower levels of that development, at the apex of which is this same human being — and if he cannot find absolute principles in himself, then in lower nature he would be even less likely to find them. Whoever does not acknowledge any other reality besides this visible reality of himself and the external world must reject any ideal content of life, any true knowledge and creativity. In such a case a person is left with only lower, bestial life.

In this life, however, happiness, even if attained, always turns out to be an illusion,[p] and since, on the other hand, the aspiration toward the higher even in the face of the realization of its unattainability nevertheless remains, becoming only the source of the greatest suffering, one's natural conclusion is that life is a game not worth a candle, and complete nothingness manifests itself as the desired ending both for the individual person and for all humankind. The avoidance of this conclusion is possible only if one acknowledges that there exists, higher than a person and external nature, another absolute, divine world, endlessly more real, rich, and alive than the world of apparent, superficial phenomena. This acknowledgment is all the more natural because a person himself in his eternal origins belongs to that transcendental world, and in the highest levels of his life and knowledge always preserves, not only a material, but also an actual link with it.

    p. Consider the joys that in life's feast
       You could drink from the cup of happiness,
       And agree, that no matter who you are in this world,
       There is something better — not to be.[16]

Concerning the Law of Historical Development

Thus the third force, which is supposed to provide for human development its absolute content, may be only the revelation of that higher divine world, and those people, that nation through which this force can manifest itself, must be only the *intermediary* between humankind and superhuman reality, the free, conscious instrument of the latter. Such a nation is not required to have any special, limited mission and is not called upon to work on the forms and elements of human existence, but instead must only convey the living soul, and provide focus and wholeness to a broken and deadened humankind through its union with purely divine principles. Such a nation needs neither some sort of special advantage nor any special strengths and external talents, for it does not act of its own volition and does not carry out its own intentions. This nation — the carrier of the third divine potential — must only be free of any exclusiveness and one-sidedness, and must be above narrow special interests; it must not direct itself with singular energy to any particular lower sphere of life and activity; it must be indifferent to this life with its petty interests, and possess a comprehensive belief in the positive reality of the higher world and a passive relationship to it. These qualities undoubtedly belong to the tribal character of the Slavic peoples, and especially to the national character of the Russian people. Historical conditions, however, do not allow us to search for another carrier of the third force, since all the remaining historical nations are subject to the predominating power of one or another of two lower exclusive potentials of human development: the historical nations of the East, to the power of the first potential, and of the West, to the power of the second. Only the Slavic peoples, especially the Russians, have remained free of these two lower principles and, consequently, may become the historical bearer of the third. Meanwhile, the two first forces closed the circle of their emergence and led the nations subservient to them to a state of spiritual death and decay.

I repeat, either this is the end of history, which is impossible according to the law of development, or, for the realization of the third stage required by this law, a kingdom of the third force is inevitable, the sole bearer of which may only be the Slavic peoples and Russian nation.[q] The

---

q. The external image of a slave, which up to now has been imprinted in our people, and the pitiful situation of Russia in economic and other respects cannot serve as a rebuttal to its calling, but instead can underscore it, since that higher force, which the Russian people must convey to humankind, is a force not of this world, and hence external wealth and order cannot have any significance.

lofty historical calling of Russia, from which its most pressing tasks derive their only significance, is a religious calling in the highest sense of the word. When the will and mind of people enter into communication with that which is eternally and truly existent, only then will all the particular forms and elements of life and knowledge attain their positive significance and worth; they will all be necessary organs and instruments of a single, integral life. Their contradictions and hostilities, based on the exclusive self-affirmation of each person, will necessarily disappear as soon as all people together freely subordinate themselves to an indivisible principle and focus.

From this it is not difficult to detect what would happen, in particular, to the component elements determined by us of the universal human organism in its third, final state. All the spheres and levels of this organism must be found here, as stated, in a completely free internal combination, or synthesis. To be of this kind, this synthesis must exclude the simple, absolute equality of spheres and levels: they are not equal, but of equal worth, i.e., each of them is equally necessary for the completely integrated fullness of the organism, although their special significance in it is indeed varied, to the extent that they must exist among themselves in a definite relationship conditioned by the particular character of each one. The universal human organism is a complex organism. First and foremost, three higher levels of its general or ideal existence — specifically mysticism in the sphere of creative work, theology in the sphere of knowledge, and the church in the sphere of social life — together form an organic whole that may be called by the old name "religion" (insofar as it serves as the connecting means between the human and divine worlds). But subsequently each member of this whole unites with the lower levels of the sphere corresponding to it, and together with these levels forms a particular organization. Thus in the first case, mysticism in an internal connection with the remaining levels of creative work, specifically with the fine arts and with technical art, forms a single organic whole whose unity, like the unity of any organism, consists of a common goal, whereas their peculiarities and differences are made up of the means or instruments appropriate for its attainment. The goal as such is defined only by the higher level, while the means is defined together with the lower levels. The goal here is mystical — the interaction with a higher world by means of inner creative activity. Contributing to the attainment of this goal is not only the direct means of a mystical character, but likewise genuine art, and genuine technical, applied art* (especially since all three have the same origin — inspiration). This relationship in the sphere of creative work differs from that of the first stage of development in the fact that at that time the subordinate levels, not being detached from the first (whose detachment was completed only during the second phase of development), properly speaking, and not actually existing as such, consequently could not serve a higher purpose consciously and freely, i.e., of their own volition. If we called this first substantial unity of creativity, immersed in mysticism, "theurgy," let us call this new organic or its multifaceted unity "free theurgy" or "integral creativity."

To continue, the second member of the religious whole — theology — in a harmonious union with philosophy and science forms *free theosophy* or *integral knowledge*. In the primitive state of the universal human spirit (in the first stage of development), philosophy and science, not existing independently, could not serve as actual instruments of theology. For theology the enormous significance of independent philosophy, having elaborated its own forms of cognition, and independent science, furnished with complex instruments of observation and experimentation and enriched by vast amounts of empirical and historical material, is readily apparent, when both of these forces, having freed themselves of the exclusivity or egotism that is fatal for themselves, reach the point of conscious necessity to use everything in their means to attain the common, supreme goal of cognition as defined by theology. Moreover, the latter in its turn will have to reject the unlawful pretension to regulate the very means of philosophical cognition and limit the very material of science, interfering in their private area of concern, such as was the case with the theology of the Middle Ages. Only the kind of theology that is grounded in independent philosophy and science may, along with them, be transformed into free theosophy, since only those who grant freedom to others are free themselves.

Finally, normal relations in the social sphere are determined by the fact that the higher level of this sphere or third member of the religious whole — spiritual society or the church — forms in a free internal union with the political and economic societies a single integral organism: a *free*

---

*The word *technika* in the original refers to what might be called "technical, applied art," having to do with expert craftsmanship and even technological skill. It is related to τέχνη, which has the connotation of "manual skill or craft." Plato, however, applied it to loftier skills, such as "political art" or "poetic art."

theocracy or *integral society*. The church as such does not interfere in governmental and economic matters, but provides for the government and district council a higher purpose and absolute norms for their activities. In other words, the government and district council are completely free in the allocation of their own resources and forces, as long as they have in mind upon doing so those higher requirements by which spiritual society defines itself — a society that in this manner, like a divine being, must move everything, while itself remaining unmovable.[r]

Thus all spheres and levels of universal human existence in this third, final phase of historical development will have to form an organic whole, singular in its origin and purpose, and many-tripled in its organs and members. The normal correlative activity of all the organs forms a new, common sphere — that of *integral life*. The bearer of this life in humankind may be *at first*, as we have seen, only the Russian people. During the time that history was determined by the activities of other forces, Russia could only instinctively, without any consciousness of it, wait for her calling; it goes without saying that she will not accept it all at once, but initially will take it on only through a more narrow union, a brotherhood or society in the midst of the Russian people. But since integral, synthetic life in its essence is free of any exclusivity or national one-sidedness, it will necessarily spread as well to the rest of humankind, when the latter by the very course of history will be forced to reject its old, outdated principles and consciously submit to new and higher ones. Only this life, this culture, which does not exclude anything, but in its uni-totality combines a higher level of unity with a fuller development of free multiplicity* — only this life may provide a genuine, solid satisfaction of all the requirements of human feeling, thought, and will, and may be, in this manner, genuinely universal, or universal and cultural. In the light

---

r. I will note in passing that if all governmental or political activity, based on right and law, has specifically a male character, economic or household activity indisputably belongs to women. As in a personal union — the family — the housekeepers were always women, so they specifically should be the keepers of world society. Herein lies the natural kinship between socialism and the so-called woman's question, and the necessary future transformation of a social democracy into a gynecocracy.

*One of the tenets of Orthodox Christianity: the concept of *sobornost'* (Russ.), translated as "communitarianism." In communitarianism the individual retains his identity along with his obligations to the collective whole. The harmoniously functioning community corresponds with the Orthodox idea of *simfonia* (Russ.), a symphony of individuals. See I. A. Esaulov, *Kategoriia sobornosti v russkoi literature* (The category of communitarianism in Russian literature) (Petrozavodsk: izdatel'stvo Petrozavodskogo universiteta, 1995).

Concerning the Law of Historical Development

of this it is clear that concomitantly and especially as a consequence of its uni-totality, this culture will be more than human, since it will lead people into an actual interaction with the divine world.

Thus the final phase of historical development, constituting a common goal for humankind, is expressed in the formation of a uni-total, vital organization that is supposed to give objective satisfaction to all the fundamental needs and aspirations of human nature, and is therefore directly defined as the summum bonum.[17]

The concept of a collective or social organism, like that of development, is not new, but both of these terms have never been clearly understood in their application to humankind. Usually the accepted example of the universal organism is the organism of the animal body, and moreover, between them various parallels and analogies are cited, which often border on the ridiculous. Meanwhile, an animal body is only a particular instance of an organism, and one can utilize it here only as an example for clarification, not as the basis for constructing an argument. Furthermore, the basic forms of the universal organism have never been acknowledged in their sum total and normal interrelationship; not a single existing argument has taken into account all the nine forms noted above.* Finally, the three main stages of development, in their logical commonality established by Hegel, were not definitively applied by anyone to the full development of all the fundamental spheres of the universal organism, which generally was viewed as being more static. The synthetic view elaborated here of the general history of humankind preserves the specific characteristics of the spiritual organism, without limiting it to organizations of a lower order, and defines its relations by the very idea of the organism, and not by accidental analogies concerning other lower creatures. Furthermore, the stated view does not encroach on the integrity of human nature, does not castrate it by removing one or another of its active forces; it applies the great logical law of development, in its abstractness formulated by Hegel, to the universal human organism in the sum total of its parts.

We have now received an answer to the question we posed at the beginning of this essay: it was defined as the formation of a uni-total, universal hu-

---

*These nine forms appear on p. 32 of the translated text, comprising theosophy (theology, philosophy, and science), theocracy (church, government, and economic society), and theurgy (mysticism, fine art, and technical art).

man organization in the form of integral creativity or free theurgy, integral knowledge or free theosophy, and integral society or free theocracy. For a person, genuine, objective morality consists of his contributing to this common goal consciously and freely, and identifying his personal will with it; this identification, which is also the liberation of a person, will inescapably come to pass when he genuinely acknowledges the truth of this idea. "Learn the truth, and the truth shall make you free" [John 8:32].

However, among the three general spheres of normal human existence, two in particular — free theurgy and free theocracy — are subject in their formation and development to the kind of particular conditions that cannot be found in any direct dependence on the will or activity of an isolated individual, who is inherently powerless here and can neither begin nor speed up the normal formation [of the spheres]. Only in one sphere — free theosophy or integral knowledge — does an isolated individual emerge as a genuine subject and actor, and here the personal consciousness of the idea already constitutes the beginning of its realization. In this sphere labor thus becomes the duty of everyone who has apprehended the normal purpose of human development. For this reason I, too, having come to this realization, have undertaken, to the extent of my strength and abilities, a systematic elaboration of those ideas that, according to my convictions, must lie at the basis of integral knowledge. But before proceeding to the subject proper, I must also examine the relationship of free theosophy as normal, or integral, knowledge to other one-sided, or abnormal, currents in the area of knowledge. This constitutes the subject of the next chapter.

PART II

Concerning the Three Types of Philosophy

Free theosophy is the organic synthesis of theology, philosophy, and experimental science, and only this synthesis may contain in itself the integral truth of knowledge: outside of it science, philosophy, and theology are only separate parts or aspects, detached organs of knowledge, and thus they cannot in any way be adequate for integral truth itself. Of course, one can attain an uncertain degree of synthesis by taking as a point of departure any of its components. This is because, since true science is impossible without philosophy and theology, just as true philosophy is impossible without theology and positive science, and true theology without philosophy and science, each of these elements, developed to its genuine fullness, necessarily takes on a synthetic character and becomes integral knowledge. Thus positive science, elevated to a true system or pursued analytically to its genuine origins and roots, is transformed into free theosophy; philosophy, freed of its one-sidedness, becomes free theosophy as well; and theology, freed of its exclusivity, is necessarily transformed into the same free theosophy. If the latter is generally defined as integral knowledge, in particular it must be designated as integral science or as integral philosophy; the difference here lies only in the point of departure and mode of elaboration, for the results and positive content are the same. In the present essay the point of departure is philosophical thought; free theosophy is examined here as a philosophical system, and first and foremost I must demonstrate that genuine philosophy necessarily must have this theosophical character, or that it must only be what I call "free theosophy" or "integral knowledge."

The word "philosophy," as is well known, does not have a single, definitive meaning, but is used in many various meanings that may be somewhat incompatible with each other. First of all, we encounter two main conceptions of philosophy that differ to equal degrees from each other: according to the first, philosophy is *only* a theory, is a matter *only* for academic circles; according to the second, it is more than a theory, is predominantly a matter for life, and therefore for academic circles as well. According to the first conception, philosophy relates *exclusively* to the cognition of a person; according to the second, it also addresses the higher aspirations of human will, and the higher ideals of human feeling. Thus it possesses not only theoretical but also moral and aesthetic knowledge, being situated in an internal interaction with the spheres of creativity and practical activity, although differing from them as well. For the philosophy corresponding to the first conception — philosophy for academic circles — a person is only required to have a mind developed to a certain degree, enriched by some knowledge, and liberated from vulgar prejudices. For the philosophy corresponding to the second conception — philosophy as a matter for life — a person is required, besides the above, to possess a particular inclination of the will, i.e., a particular moral temperament, as well as artistic feeling and understanding, and the power of imagination, or fantasy. The first philosophy, being concerned exclusively with theoretical questions, does not have any direct internal connection with private or social life; the second philosophy strives to become a formative and guiding force in life.

One may ask which of these two philosophies is the true one. Both possess the same claims on the knowledge of the truth, but this word itself is understood by them completely differently: for the one, it possesses only an abstract-theoretical meaning, while for the other it is living and essential. If to resolve our question we turn to the etymology of the word "philosophy," we will receive an answer in favor of living philosophy. Clearly the appellation "love of wisdom," i.e., a love for the pursuit of wisdom (such is the meaning of the Greek word φιλοσοφία), cannot be applied to abstract theoretical science. By "wisdom" is implied not only the fullness of knowledge but also a moral perfection, an inner wholeness of the spirit. In this manner the word "philosophy" signifies an aspiration for the spiritual wholeness of the human being — it was used in this meaning originally. But it goes without saying that this etymological argument in and of itself has no significance, since a word taken from a dead language may resultantly assume a meaning independent of its etymology. Thus, for example, the word "chemistry," etymologically meaning "relating to black earth" or "Egyptian" (from the word *chem* — black earth; like the personal name "Egypt"), in its contemporary meaning has of course very little in common with either black earth or Egypt. But concerning philosophy, it is worth noting that even today it is understood by the majority of people in a meaning corresponding to the original one. In both the general meaning and in its expression — colloquial language — to this day, one can call someone a "philosopher" who possesses not only little education but no education at all, if only that person possesses a particular mental and moral temperament. In this manner, not only etymology but also common usage gives this word a meaning that does not at all correspond to scholastic philosophy, but is rather close to what we termed the "philosophy for life," which of course already constitutes a big *praejudicium*[1] in favor of the latter. But this circumstance nevertheless does not have a decisive significance: the current conception of philosophy may not satisfy the demands of more developed thinking. Thus, to resolve the question in its essence we must examine the *inner* principles of both philosophies, and only by the justifiability or unjustifiability thereof we may reach a conclusion in favor of the one or the other.

The entire variety of systems in academic philosophy may be reduced to two main types or currents, concerning which some of the systems represent simple variations of these types or different stages of their development, while others form transitional steps or intermediate links from one type to another; a third group represents experiments in the electrical connection between the first two.

The views belonging to the first type understand the fundamental subject of philosophy to lie in the external world, in the sphere of material nature, and corresponding to this, consider the real source of cognition to be external experience, i.e., the experience we gain by our ordinary perceptual apparatus. Therefore, in accordance with the views of this type of philosophy, its proponents may call its posited subject "naturalism" and its posited source of cognition "external empiricism."

In acknowledging nature as the real object of philosophy, nature that we apprehend by external experience, naturalism, however, cannot attribute such significance to the direct reality that surrounds us in all the complex and changeable diversity of its phenomena. If the truth unknown to philosophy were identical with the reality surrounding us, if in this manner it were at our fingertips, there would be no reason to search for it, and philosophy as a particular branch of knowledge would not have a reason to exist. But the fact of the matter is that this reality of ours is not self-sufficient; it manifests itself as something fragmentary, changeable, and productive, and thus it requires an explanation of itself from another truly-existent* as its first principle. This phenomenal reality — what we collectively call "the world" — is only the given subject of philosophy, i.e., what needs to be explained, the task to be carried out and resolved, the riddle to be solved. The key to this task, *le mot de l'énigme*,[2] is precisely the *unknown* in philosophy. All philosophical currents, no matter where they seek existent truth, no matter how they define it, similarly acknowledge that it must manifest a universal and immutable character that distinguishes it from the transient and splintered reality of phenomena. Naturalism also acknowledges this as a philosophical view and therefore considers nature as truly existent, not in the sense of a simple aggregate of external phenomena in their visible diversity, but rather in the sense of a common, real basis or substance of these phenomena. In determining this basis, naturalism undergoes three stages of development. The first, or immature phase of naturalistic philosophy (represented, for example, by the medieval Ionian School), may be called "elementary" or "elemental" materialism: one of the so-called elements is accepted here as the basis or principle (ἀρχή), while everything else is its variant. But it is easy to see that every element, as a limited form of reality differing from everything else, cannot be an authentic first principle; the first principle can be only a general, nonspecific element or the common source of all elements (τὸ ἄπειρον of Anaximander).

This single producer of all of existence, the common mother nature *(materia* comes from *mater)*, having from itself given birth to all forms of life, cannot be found in dead and soulless reality, but rather must contain in itself all living forces of existence, must itself be living and animate. Such a view, which enlivens material nature, is called "hylozoism," and it constitutes the second stage of naturalistic philosophy (whose representatives are, incidentally, the naturalistic philosophers of the fifteenth and sixteenth centuries, the most prominent of whom was Giordano Bruno). These ideas

---

*The philosophical category Solovyov uses in the given sentence (and elsewhere in this essay), истинно-сущее, appears as a substantivized adjective, and for precision's sake I have left it in this form ("truly-existent"). No noun in English translation approximates the meaning Solovyov intends here.

about nature as a living, animate being may be entirely accurate (and consequently we will see that they are such in reality), but from the point of view of naturalism it is impossible for them to identify any sufficient foundations; these ideas may exist in naturalism only until that time when it becomes aware of a mode of cognition corresponding to it. However, as soon as the consciousness appears that if the basis of all of existence lies in the external world it may only be known by external experience — as soon as this consciousness appears, hylozoism becomes unthinkable for a naturalist. In reality, in external experience we do not find an animate nature at all as a first cause of all phenomena; in general, in external experience we find only the diverse variants and mechanical movements of matter; the active, living force that produced these movements not only does not appear in external experience, but also cannot be logically extracted from any of its forms of evidence. Thus from this point of view we may accept as the basis for all living things only the substratum of mechanical motion, i.e., the constant indivisible particles of matter — atoms.

Atoms — indivisible material particles — are authentically existent, irreplaceably present; everything else derives from the diverse mechanical combination of these atoms and is merely a transient phenomenon — such is the principle that defines the third and last stage of naturalism — mechanical materialism, or atomism. This view does not take into consideration the worldwide living force underscored by hylozoism; without the acknowledgment of a force *in general,* mechanical materialism, too, cannot get along; it must acknowledge at least the partial elementary forces inherent in atoms. Thus, the conviction emerges that all of existence consists of force and matter — *Kraft und Stoff.* If we set aside some misunderstandings that have to do more with words than deeds, we will have to agree with this basic principle of materialism. In reality, everything *consists* of force and matter. The truth and simplicity of this conviction gained for materialism its enormous popularity through the ages, but on the other hand, it could never satisfy to any degree deep-thinking philosophical minds. The reason for this is clear: in speaking the truth, materialism is not speaking the entire truth. It is just as true that the universe consists of force and matter as it is that the *Venus de Milo* is made of marble, and just as the latter assertion is of no significance for an artist, so the former is not worth anything to a philosopher. It goes without saying that the very question of a common substratum for all of existence is of incomparably greater significance for philosophy than the question concerning the material of a statue for art; but here I have in mind the answer of a materialist to this important question — the answer is completely indefinite and vapid in its generality. Whenever materialism tries to avoid this generality and attach some sort of positive definitions to its principle, it meets a rather unfortunate fate.

Materialism defines matter as an aggregate of atoms. But what are atoms? For the naturalist they are empirically given particles, relatively indivisible, i.e., we cannot by any means divide them under existing conditions. In this manner, in answer to the question, "What is matter?" we receive the thoughtful response, "Matter is the aggregate of particles of matter." But those few materialists who feel a certain dissatisfaction with this answer resort to another means of definition, namely, the analysis of the *qualitative* elements of matter. Setting aside all the particular and secondary characteristics, this analysis reduces matter to impenetrability, i.e., to the ability to exert resistance to an external action. Properly speaking, here we can speak only about resistance to *our* action. The resistance we feel creates a general impression of materiality, and since all secondary and particular manifestations of matter, regardless of their color, sound, etc., are also subject to our sensations — visual, auditory, etc. — in general the entire empirical content of matter is nothing other than our sensation. Such a conclusion clearly destroys the point of view of naturalism, transferring the origin of all of existence from the external world to us. To avoid this, materialism must return to the concept of atoms, but no longer as empirical particles of matter, reduced to our sensations; rather, atoms become absolutely indivisible, real points that exist in and of themselves, independent of every type of experience, and conversely, by their action on a subject produce every experience. Such metaphysical atoms, by their very definition as absolutely indivisible particles, cannot be found empirically, because in empiricism we have only relative, not absolute, being; if they cannot be given *empirically*, the acknowledgment of them must have logical bases and be subject to *logical* criticism. But this criticism not only does not find sufficient logical bases for the confirmation of such absolutely indivisible and concomitantly material points, but with complete obviousness demonstrates the logical impossibility of such a notion.

Actually these atoms either are of a certain length, or are not. In the first case, they are divisible, and as a result are only empirical, and not genuine, atoms. If they inherently do not have any length (which should already be the case because length is a property of empirical, phenomenal matter stipulated by forms of subjective perception), then they are mathematical points; but for them to be the origin of all of existence, these mathematical points must possess their own substantiality. This substantiality cannot be material, because all the properties of matter, not excluding length, are taken away from atoms and the entire material world is acknowledged as phenomenal, not substantial. Consequently, this substantiality, not being material, must be *dynamic*. Atoms are not component parts of matter, but *forces* that create matter. These forces by their interaction (among themselves) and their combined action upon our subject create our whole empirical reality, the entire world of phenomena. In this matter it is not force that is a property of matter, as was supposed at first, but on the contrary, matter is the creator of forces or, more precisely, the relative limit of their interaction. Thus atoms either do not exist at all or are immaterial dynamic units, living monads. With this conclusion mechanical materialism finally declines, and along with it the entire naturalistic worldview. In reality, after the equation of atoms with live forces, two paths remain open for thinkers of a naturalistic bent. Having acknowledged the reality of monads, one could turn to the investigation of their internal content and mutual relationships. Such an investigation is necessarily of a speculative character (since monads are not givens in the experiment), going outside the boundaries of naturalism; it leads us, as will be shown subsequently, into the very depths of mystical philosophy. The other path would be to remain at all costs in the territory of empiricism, to accept all the negative consequences necessarily deriving from this point of view. Specifically: if the only source of cognition is external experience, and if in external experience we are not given any origins of being, or any forms of essence, but instead are given only phenomena reduced to our sensations and conceptions, these phenomena in their relationship to continuity and similarity must then be recognized as the sole object of cognition. Mechanical materialism, however, depending as well on external experience exclusively, allows something that is not present in external experience, namely, atoms. Such a contradiction must be eliminated; one should reject even such pitiful forms of essence as atoms, one should reject all kinds of essence, offering them all as a sacrifice to empiricism, with which a naturalistic point of view is inextricably linked, since the latter does not have any other suitable means of cognition than external empiricism.

Thus naturalism must acknowledge as the sole object of cognition that which is given in actual external experience, i.e., phenomena in their external link of continuity and similarity. But the study of phenomena in this sense is a matter for the positive sciences, of which consistent naturalism thus becomes a part, no longer being philosophy. It avoided hyperphysics only to be engulfed in its entirety by empiricism and to merge with the positive sciences. For many people such a result is an expression of real truth, the ultimate triumph of human reason over the foggy specters of metaphysics. Instead of the essence of phenomena, instead of reasons and goals, positive sciences emerge — the immutable laws of phenomena, instead of transcendental philosophy. Empiricism sees its complete triumph in such a substitution, which for it, to be sure, is a triumph of truth over delusions. What is unfortunate is that the inexorable logic of the intellect does not allow empiricism any peace even in this minor, but evidently completely harmless, refuge of positive science; it irrepressibly pushes it into the dark abyss of absolute skepticism. In reality, science strives to learn the laws of phenomena, i.e., the necessary and universal relationships among them — relationships common to all homogeneous phenomena in all specific cases, past and future, i.e., throughout the ages. It is supposed that science will discover these laws from experimentation. But in experiments we can observe only the empirical relationships of phenomena, i.e., their relationships in given instances subject to our experience. The well-known relationship of consistency and similarity among given phenomena, similar in all our past experiments, is a fact. But what can vouch for the immutability of this relationship through the ages absolutely, both in the years subsequent to and in those preceding our experiments, in which, consequently, we cannot confirm this relationship in the guise of a fact? What gives the empirical, factual connection among phenomena the character of universality and necessity? What makes this connection a law? Our scientific experience has existed, one may say, since yesterday, and the number of instances subject to it, in comparison with the rest, is infinitely small. But even if this experience had existed for millions of centuries, these millions would also not be of any significance with respect to the endless time ahead of us, and consequently could not at all facilitate the absolute certitude of the laws discovered in this experience.

Here we must establish something completely inconceivable: Those same contemporary empiricists who laugh so much at the scholastics who affirm in the form of axioms that nature does not tolerate a vacuum, does not make rapid changes, and the like, themselves proclaim completely seriously that universality and necessity — in other words, the immutability of the laws of phenomena — are based on the axiom that nature is constant and uniform in its actions. If the laughable scholastics had the right to affirm such axioms, because they generally acknowledged *veritates aeternae et universales*,[3] then what attribute can we attach to these contemporary empiricists who, in negating all sorts of a priori truths, meanwhile serve us such pure *veritatem aeternam* concerning nature and its actions? And, moreover, what exactly does nature constitute for the empiricist? There exists a general conception of it, abstracted from phenomena and their laws and consequently not having any content of its own that is independent of these phenomena and laws. Thus the axiom of the constancy of nature is reduced to the affirmation that the laws of phenomena are immutable, and we receive the most pure *idem per idem*:[4] the immutability of the laws of phenomena, based on the simple affirmation of this very same immutability.

Thus, in answer to the question, "Why does a certain given relationship in an experiment become a general and necessary law?" the empiricist is left with one answer: "Because to date this relationship has always been observed." But in such a case this is a law only until the first observation that can show a different relationship among phenomena of this type; consequently, this is no longer a legitimate law that is general and necessary. If we allow that a given relationship is a law, because it is inherently necessary, i.e., a priori, we are already moving out of empiricism and into speculative philosophy. Thus from the empirical point of view even the cognition of phenomena in their general, necessary laws is impossible; consistent empiricism destroys not only philosophy, but also positive science in its theoretical meaning. What remains is only the possibility of empirical information about phenomena in their given factual connection, which is changeable and transient — information that could be of practical use, but that obviously is deprived of any theoretical interest.

Empiricism allows the cognition only of phenomena. But what is a phenomenon? It is opposed to what is real in itself, and consequently is defined as that which is not contained within itself, but which exists only with respect to another, specifically with respect to us as the cognizing subject. All phenomena are reduced to our sensations or, more precisely, to various states of our cognition. Everything we usually accept as external objects independent of us, everything we see, hear, touch, etc., consists in reality of our own sensations, i.e., of the alterations of our subject, and consequently cannot have any claims on some other kind of reality besides the one that all the other alterations of the subject have in some way: desires, feelings, thoughts, etc. Thus the juxtaposition of internal and external experience disappears; it is no longer possible to speak of external objects and our psychic states as things opposed to each other, since external objects, too, are in reality our psychic states and nothing more — everything can be similarly considered a phenomenon, i.e., an alteration of our subject, various states of our consciousness. This refers not only to so-called inanimate objects, but also to the presupposed objects outside us. Everything that we can know about other people is reduced to our own sensations: we see people, we hear them, we know palpably how we see and hear them, and we touch other external objects. In this relationship — in the relationship of the means of our knowledge of them [of external objects] — between people and other objects there is no difference, and if, as is the case with empiricism, we can extract from the means of cognition the conclusion about the form of existence of what is knowable from the notion that this material object *is known* to me by my sensations, in order to conclude that it also *consists* only of my sensations, then such a conclusion must be applicable to people as well. I know about other people only by my sensations; they exist for me only in these states of my consciousness; therefore, they are nothing other than the states of my consciousness. But I also know about my own self as a subject only in the states of my consciousness, and therefore I myself, too, as a subject must be reduced to the states of my own consciousness. But this is absurd, since *my* consciousness already presupposes *me*. What remains, therefore, is to allow that phenomena of consciousness exist, but not of my own, since I do not exist, but of consciousness in general, without one who is conscious, and likewise without one who is knowable. Phenomena exist inherently, impressions exist inherently. But this directly contradicts the logical sense of these terms. A phenomenon, in opposition to what is real, means only that which does not exist in and of itself, but rather exists only for another; the same holds true for an impression as well. If this other — what is represented — does not exist, then the representation does not exist, either, the phenomenon as well does not exist, and then everything is reduced to some kind of undifferentiated being that is self-contained and has no relationship to another (since the other does not exist) — a conclusion that is logically absurd and has nothing in common with empirical reality, a concept by which, consequently, empiricism is ultimately destroyed.

Concerning the Three Types of Philosophy

To avoid such a conclusion one must acknowledge that the cognizing subject as such possesses not phenomenal but absolute being, and is not a phenomenon but the truly-existent. Such an assertion represents the beginning of a second current or type of academic philosophy that is usually designated by the term "idealism." Here the truly-existent is no longer posited in the external world, where naturalism seeks it, but in us ourselves — in the cognizing subject. The resultant empiricism, which is aware of itself and has engulfed the principle of naturalism through the information of every external material form of being acting upon the sensations of the subject, thus constitutes a natural transition from naturalism to idealism.

If we affirm that the cognizing subject possesses absolute being, idealism, to be sure, has in mind not empirical subjects in their concrete multiplicity, in particular, isolated acts of their materially conditioned cognition; it has in mind the cognizing subject as such, i.e., in the general and necessary forms of its cognition, or *in its ideas* (hence the term "idealism"). These ideas, as universal and necessary ones, evidently cannot be given empirically; they are accessible only to the a priori thinking of pure reason; for this reason idealism with respect to the mode of cognition is necessarily pure rationalism. (As is well known, this view was developed with the greatest conscientiousness and purity in the newest Germanic philosophy, which originated with Kant. The development of this philosophy is well known to all of us, and I shall only remind us of it here in a few words.) The truly-existent for idealism is that which is known by pure thought, but only general concepts are apprehended by pure thought; the idea relates to this, insofar as it is given in pure, rational thought. Thus, the truly-existent is a general concept, and since all of existence must be a manifestation of the truly-existent as a universal source, all of existence is nothing other than the development of a general concept, but the latter, as the general concept κατ' ἐξοχήν, can only be that which does not contain in itself any concrete content, i.e., the conception of pure *being*, decisively not containing anything in itself, not being distinguished in any way from the conception *nothing*, and consequently equivalent to it. Thus rationalistic idealism approaches the absolute logic of Hegel, according to which all of existence is the result of the self-development of this pure conception of being, equivalent to nothing.

If everything possesses authentic existence only in its conception, then the cognizing subject, too, is nothing other than a conception, and in this relationship does not have any advantage over the rest of being. Thus concepts or ideas, forming all of existence, are not ideas of a thinking subject (it itself is only an idea) — they are in and of themselves, and all of existence is, to repeat, the result of their self-development or, more precisely, the self-development of a single concept — pure being or nothingness. In other words, everything derives from nothing or everything in its essence is nothing. Everything is a pure thought, i.e., a thought without a thinker and without that which is thought, an act without an actor and without an object of the action.[a] Here we see a striking example of how currents directly opposed to each other come together in their most extreme conclusions. In reality, consistent empiricism leads, as we have seen, to a similar result — to the acknowledgment of a representation without a representer and without that which is represented, to the acknowledgment of states of consciousness without a conscious subject and without that which is conceived — in short, phenomena without the existent — and to the acknowledgment of some sort of undifferentiated, flowing being. The difference lies only in the fact that empiricism defines this being sensually, as sensation or sense impressions, while panlogism defines it rationally, as a general concept. But this difference only seems to exist, because if everything is considered a sensation and, on the other hand, if everything is considered a conception, both sensation and conception lose their specificity, their characteristic significance. A sensation that is everything is no longer a sensation, and a conception that is everything is no longer a conception — the difference exists only in words. Both the one and the other, deprived of a subject and object, become diffused into absolute indefiniteness, into pure nothingness. It is their reduction to zero (which they themselves bring about) that is a sufficient refutation of these one-sided views. And if this self-destruction of theirs issues (however indisputably) from a logical course of thought leading to necessary investigations, which are already contained in the points of departure or premises of these views, then clearly their delusion consists of these same premises.

The major premise of empirical naturalism maintains that the truly-existent is found in the external world, in nature, and that the means of its cognition is external experience. The major premise of rationalistic idealism maintains that the truly-existent is found in the cognizing subject, in

---

a. Logical necessity, leading the resultant idealism to zero, was explicated by many thinkers, for example (to note the latter), Hartmann in his *Grundlesung des transcendentalen Realismus*.[5] Only the brain-dead dogmatists of Hegelianism can deny this necessity.

Concerning the Three Types of Philosophy

our reason, and that the means of its cognition is pure, rational thought or the construction of general concepts. Meanwhile, in the course of the consistent development of these points of departure, empiricism leads to the negation of the internal world, nature, and external experience as a means of knowing that which is existent, while rationalism leads to the negation of the cognizing subject and pure thought as a means of knowing what is existent (insofar as what is existent negates itself). Thus in repudiating the principles of both of these currents or types of philosophy, we are not in need of any arguments external to them: they refute themselves when they reach their final, logical conclusion, and along with these currents the entire abstract scholastic philosophy, of which they represent the two indispensable poles, falls apart.

Thus, either one must reject genuine cognition in general and assume the point of view of absolute skepticism,[b] or one must acknowledge that the unknown of philosophy consists neither of the real being of the external world nor of the ideal being of our reason, and that it cannot be known by way of empiricism or by way of rational thought. In other words, one must acknowledge that the truly-existent possesses its own absolute reality, which is completely independent of the reality of the external, material world and of our thought, and, in the opposite direction, communicates its reality to this world and its ideal content to our thought. The views that attribute to the truly-existent such a supercosmic and superhuman origin, and moreover, not in the form only of an abstract principle (as it appears, for example, in Cartesian and Wolffian* deism) but also in all the fullness of its living reality — such views go beyond the bounds of scholastic philosophy, and along with its two types they form a specific third type of mental contemplation, usually known as *mysticism*.

According to this view, truth is contained neither in the logical form of knowing nor in its empirical content; in general, it does not belong to theoretical knowledge in its separateness or exclusiveness — such knowledge is not genuine. Knowledge of truth is only that which corresponds to the will for good and to the feeling for beauty. Although the definition of truth re-

---

b. Skepticism is a simple negation of every kind of *specific* philosophy (insofar as doubt constitutes *negation*, specifically the negation of certitude and determination), and for this reason there is no basis for considering it (as many do) a particular type or current of philosophy.

*Christian Wolff (1679-1754), Polish-German philosopher, whose ideas on the rational soul would subsequently be refuted by Kant.

lates directly to the sphere of knowledge but not at all to its exclusiveness (which already is not truth), this definition must belong to knowledge only insofar as it agrees with the other spheres of spiritual being, in other words: what is true in the genuine sense of this word may be only that which concomitantly is the good and beauty. To be sure, there exist so-called truths that are accessible to a cognizing ability in its isolation and abstraction; such, on the one hand, are truths that are purely formal, and on the other, truths that are purely material or empirical. A given mathematical proposition may possess formal truth without any direct relationship to will and feeling, but in return it is inherently deprived of any reality or real content. On the other hand, a given historical fact or fact of the natural sciences may possess material truth without any relationship to ethics or aesthetics, but in return it is inherently deprived of any reasonable meaning. Truths of the first kind are unreal, those of the second kind are unreasonable; those of the first kind are in need of realization, while those of the second kind are in need of comprehension. Genuine truth, integral and vital, contains both its own reality and its own reasonableness, and superimposes these qualities onto everything else. In accordance with this, the subject of mystical philosophy is neither the world of phenomena, related to our sensations, nor the world of ideas, related to our thoughts, but rather the living reality of beings in their internal, living relations; this philosophy is concerned not with the external order of phenomena, but with the internal order of beings and their life, which is determined by their relation to the original entity. To be sure, mysticism, too, like every philosophy, is moved by ideas and thoughts, but it is known that these thoughts have meaning only insofar as they relate to what is conceived through them and what already by itself is not thought, but constitutes more than thought. Academic philosophy either mixes what is existent with one or another form of being, i.e., of representations, or negates the very knowability of what is existent. Mystical philosophy, on the one hand, accepts that any kind of being is only a means of representing what is existent, and is not itself that which is existent; on the other hand, in opposition to skeptical assertions that a person cannot know anything except for representations, this philosophy posits that since a person is more than a representation or being, he may thus, without even going outside of himself, know about the existent.

Mysticism consists of a sphere of possible philosophical views, since it is clear that the unknown of philosophy may possess its existence either in the external world, i.e., in the known object as such, or in us, the cognizing subject as such, or in itself independently of us or the external world. A fourth supposition would be inconceivable. If the first two views, which constitute academic philosophy, cannot be accepted because they cancel each other out, then we are left either to reject in general the search for truth or to accept this third view *as the basis* of genuine philosophy. If truth, in being located neither in the external world nor in us ourselves, may *eo ipso*[6] belong only to the proper transcendental reality of the absolute first principle, and if nevertheless, as skepticism concludes, we cannot cognize this transcendental reality, then it means that in general we cannot know the truth. Thus the arguments of skepticism against the possibility of mystical philosophy by this same argument militate against every search for truth, against all types of philosophy, and ultimately against all types of knowledge.

Thus, mystical knowledge[c] is necessary for philosophy, since without this knowledge, in consistent empiricism and in logical rationalism similarly, it leads to absurdity. But this mystical knowledge may be only *the basis* for genuine philosophy, in a similar manner to how external experience serves as the basis for empirical philosophy and logical thinking as the basis of rationalism; however, in and of itself mystical knowledge does not yet form a system of genuine or synthetic philosophy, of what I have called "integral knowledge" or "free theosophy." By its very conception this system must be free of any exclusiveness or one-sidedness, while mysticism, taken separately, perhaps in reality is exclusive, in emphasizing only one direct kind of knowledge that has the form of internal absolute certitude. It goes without saying that genuine knowledge as well must be based on such certitude, but to be complete or integral it must not stop here (as does exclusive mysticism): it is also necessary for it, first, to be subject to the reflexes of reason, to receive the justification of logical thought, and second, to receive confirmation from empirical facts. In repudiating the false principles and absurd conclusions of empiricism and rationalism, genuine philosophy must contain the objective content of these currents as secondary, or subordinate, elements. This is because if integral knowledge in general is the synthesis of philosophy with theology and science, then evidently this broad synthesis must be preceded by a narrower synthesis corresponding to it in the area of philosophy among its three currents: mysticism, rationalism, and empiricism. The analogy here is indisputable:

---

c. At the moment I am utilizing this term only in its negative connotation; its positive content can be revealed only at a later time [in this essay — trans.].

mysticism corresponds to theology, and empiricism to positive science, while rationalism is associated with a strictly philosophical, abstract character since it limits itself to pure philosophical thought, at the same time that mysticism seeks support in the data of religion, and empiricism in the data of positive science. In the system of integral knowledge or free theosophy the interdependent relationship of the three philosophical elements is defined by the indicated analogy. In its absolute character mysticism is of preeminent significance, defining the supreme principle and final goal of philosophical knowledge; empiricism by its material character serves as an external basis and also as the last application or realization of the highest principles; and finally, the rationalistic, strictly philosophical element in its predominantly formal character manifests itself as the means or common link of the entire system.

From the above it is clear that free theosophy or integral knowledge is not one of the currents or types of philosophy, but rather must represent the highest state of philosophy, both in the internal synthesis of its three main currents — mysticism, rationalism, and empiricism — and similarly in its more general and broad link with theology and positive science.[d] Obeying the general law of historical development, philosophy passes through three main stages that completely correspond to those that were indicated in the first chapter [of this essay] for the entire sphere of knowledge (and for the other spheres as well). The first stage is characterized by the exclusive predominance of mysticism, which retains in a latent form or a state of fusion rational and empirical elements (which corresponds with the general predominance of theology). In the second stage these elements become isolated, and philosophy disintegrates into three separate currents or types that strive for absolute self-affirmation and consequently mutual negation; here, according to the general disintegration of the theoretical sphere into three branches hostile to each other — theology, abstract philosophy, and positive science — we have one-sided mysticism, one-sided rationalism, and one-sided empiricism. In the third stage they arrive at an internal free synthesis, which forms the basis of the general synthesis of the three levels of knowledge, and consequently also the universal synthesis of human life. If unity in the sphere of knowledge that is determined neces-

---

    d. Free theosophy thus represents a positive antithesis to skepticism: as the latter is the negation of any definite philosophy, so it [free theosophy — trans.] is the entire unity of all of them [philosophies — trans.].

sarily by a theological or mystical principle is what we generally call "theosophy" (i.e., more precisely, knowledge in its unity is theosophy), then the highest synthetic unity of the third stage (in contrast to what is not free or is fused in the first stage) is characterized by what I call "free theosophy" or "integral knowledge."

According to the general definition, the object of integral knowledge is truly-existent both in and of itself and in its relationship to the empirical reality of the subjective and objective worlds, of which it is the absolute first principle. Precisely from this emerges the division of the entire philosophical system of integral knowledge into three organic components. This is because as soon as in an object of philosophy two elements are given, specifically the absolute first principle and the secondary reality that arises from it, these two elements may be conceivable only in three relations. First, in spontaneous unity; second, in opposition; and third, in actual, distinct unity or synthesis. Thus we receive three philosophical sciences: the first examines the absolute principle in its own general and necessary (and consequently a priori) attributes, in which another, ultimate existence is contained only potentially — the stage of spontaneous unity. The second science examines the absolute principle in its role of creating or positing outside of itself a final reality — the stage of disintegration. The third science has as its subject the absolute principle as reuniting with itself the final world in actual synthetic union. This triple separation of philosophy, resulting from its very nature, has an ancient origin and in one form or another is found in all completed and at least to some degree well-conceived systems, since each separate system, being actually only a one-sided manifestation of one or another stage of philosophical knowledge, in this context aspires with its limited point of view to represent the whole of philosophy.[e]

I retain the traditional appellations for the three constituent parts of free theosophy: logic, metaphysics, and ethics. To distinguish these constituent parts from the corresponding parts of other philosophical systems, I shall use the following terms: "organic logic," "organic metaphysics," and "organic ethics."[f] According to the internal order of ideas, the exposition of the system begins with logic, to which we now must turn our attention.

---

e. In particular this must be said about the philosophy of Hegel, which in its sphere of formal, purely logical thought is completely brim-full and closed. For this reason the general formulas of Hegelianism will remain as permanent formulas of philosophy.

f. The specific meaning of these terms will be clarified at the appropriate time.

PART III

Principles of Organic Logic: Characterization of Integral Knowledge — Point of Departure and Method of Organic Logic

Organic logic in its overall character presents two different sides and must receive its *most precise* definition from two general points of view. First, it must be examined with respect to the entire system of integral knowledge or free theosophy, of which it represents the first part, and second, it must be characterized with respect to every other kind of logic, to everything that bears this name. In other words, being *theosophical logic,* it must be examined from the point of view of *theosophy* in general and from the point of view of *logic* in general.

From the first point of view, i.e., as theosophical knowledge, organic logic is characterized by the following seven points of departure:

1. by the *subject* of cognition
2. by the *goal*
3. by the general *material*
4. by its *form*
5. by the *active source* or *generative cause* of cognition *(causa efficiens)*
6. by its *point of departure*
7. by the *method* of its development or construction

As a well-known, definite division of theosophy, organic logic presents, on the one hand, well-known generic traits that determine its general-theosophical character, traits that are thus essentially identical to those of the two remaining divisions of theosophy; on the other hand, it must possess special features that distinguish it from the other two theosophical disciplines. Among the seven relationships listed above, the first five embrace the general features of integral knowledge in all its aspects: subject, goal, material, form, and active source of cognition are essentially identical in theosophical logic, metaphysics, and ethics, and the peculiarities of these sciences are determined by the differences among their points of departure and methods of development. For this reason, in examining the first five relationships, we will discuss the kind of cognition in free theosophy in general, without the differences among its aspects.

The subject of free theosophy is the *truly-existent* (τὸ ὄντως ὄν, *das wahrhaft Seiende*) *in its objective expression* or idea; in this respect as well, on the one hand, it differs decisively from empiricism, rationalism, and mysticism in their one-sidedness, while on the other hand it contains their entire objective content. It differs from empiricism insofar as the latter presupposes as its genuine subject of cognition, not the existent, which it considers completely unknowable, but only phenomena or factual (gained from experience) relationships, which, as we saw in the previous chapter, in the course of consistent development lead to internal contradiction. Concerning one-sided rationalism, it acknowledges as the subject of philosophy, not the existent as an idea, but rather the idea in and of itself, and arrives at the same negative result. Finally, one-sided mysticism underscores the existent as the subject of true cognition, but the existent only in its immediate substantiality is accessible only to the same immediate feeling or belief. Mysticism either ignores or decisively rejects the objective development of the existent as an idea, reducing the entire subjective, ideal content of knowledge to a subjective phantom of the human mind, which obviously leads to the rejection of any type of philosophy and to absolute skepticism. Free theosophy, by definition of its subject, in acknowledging along with mysticism the unconditional primary reality of the existent, deduces from this acknowledgment what it logically consists of and what is ignored by mysticism, namely, if the existent possesses unconditional reality and is absolute, i.e., all-encompassing, then it cannot exclude any type of content, neither the content of our reasoning thought nor the content of our experiences. For this reason, free theosophy, being based along with mysticism on the unconditional direct reality of the existent, acknowledges and cognizes the development of this reality in the ideas of reason and the ideas of nature, thus capturing as well what is objective in rationalism and empiricism.

Concerning the *goal* of true philosophy, it is completely rejected by rationalism, which considers philosophical cognition its own goal as a superlative form of spiritual activity. And in reality, insofar as philosophy represents the satisfaction of the theoretical requirement of knowledge, it is inherently a goal. But this same theoretical requirement is only partial, one of many, and a person has a general, higher requirement for an all-encompassing or absolute life, for which everything else, and consequently philosophy as well, may be only the means. This absolute eternal life, which in and of itself constitutes the highest good and bliss, obviously is possible only when a person does not submit to any external conditions that are foreign to him, and does not have any external, involuntary defining influences, since every such influence is suffering, in precisely the same way as suffering, objectively speaking, is nothing other than an involuntary submission to something external. However, a person evidently can free himself from what is external, which is stronger than he, only by uniting internally with that which *inherently*, in its very essence, is *free* from everything that is external, containing everything in itself, and consequently not having anything outside itself — in other words, a person must be really free only in his internal union with the truly-existent, i.e., in genuine religion. This liberation of a person from the external and the evils and sufferings connected with it, this union with the wholly-existent, or realization of genuine religion, constitutes the real goal of all normal human activities, and consequently of genuine philosophy as well, which thus is not subordinated by some other *particular* activities, but together with them serves a single absolute goal. The union of a person with the absolute as the goal of genuine knowledge acknowledges mysticism as well, but as a result of his one-sided understanding of the absolute he also understands the union with himself in a one-sided way, specifically as a confluence or absorption, in which the world disappears for a person and a person disappears for himself, which leads logically to complete annihilation, to Buddhist nirvana. However, annihilation is not freedom, it is not bliss (since to attain freedom or bliss the existence of *the free* and *the blissful* is necessary), and consequently it cannot be a goal. Freedom is might, and a genuine goal is victory and power over the external world. In a certain sense this acknowledges empiricism as well, which already in the person of its father Francis Bacon sees in knowledge one of the greatest means to might or power over nature. But for real, complete freedom a person must have power not only over the natural, external world, but also over his own; this inner power cannot be given by that knowledge to which empiricism limits itself. But in the exact same way a person cannot attain this inner freedom, or this power over his own nature from out of his own self, since he is not free — this would be tantamount to lifting oneself up by the hair. To be internally free, a person must transfer his center of human existence from his own to another, higher nature; the abstract elevation over lower nature in the name of one's own *I*, of personal dignity, and the like may be only a jump upward, after which inevitably comes a fall. Thus the goal of genuine philosophy is — to promote in its sphere, i.e., in the sphere of knowledge, the displacement of the center of human existence from its own given nature to the absolute, transcendental world, in other words — to promote a person's internal union with the truly-existent.

It goes without saying, generally speaking, that the goal of philosophy may be only the knowledge of truth, but the point is that this very truth, genuine, whole truth, necessarily is also the good, beauty, and might, and for this reason real philosophy is inextricably linked with genuine creative work and with moral activity, which give a person victory over lower nature and power over it. By itself philosophy cannot give a person either bliss or higher power, but real philosophy, i.e., integral knowledge, which is free theosophy, *cannot* be separate from other spiritual spheres; together with them it attains that higher goal, and like a necessary part of a common-human whole, by its own particular development and perfection brings about the perfection of this whole, on which, in its turn, it itself is dependent. Thus, although free theosophy may assume the origin of its development to lie inside its theoretical sphere, it may accomplish this development only jointly and simultaneously with the development of free theurgy and theocracy. *Sapienti sat.*[1]

The *material* of integral knowledge is obtained through *experience*. Usually experience is considered to be either external or internal. But, properly speaking, experience is a *contradictio in adjecto*. By a verbal definition experience is that which is experienced by a subject; it can evidently experience only that which in one way or another is found within itself, which exists for itself. And really, everything that is called "external experience," everything that relates to so-called external objects, in its material content can be reduced to our sensations, i.e., to facts of our internal consciousness, to the givens of our psychic life. Every confirmation of our external existence is already our own conclusion based on these givens, although, it goes without saying, a conclusion that is "not discursive or abstract, but intuitive and completely spontaneous." But in the entire aggregate of the givens of our psychic life or the states of our consciousness we clearly distinguish three categories: first, the states of consciousness in which we feel that we are defined by something external to ourselves, although with respect to this same external entity, as indicated, we cannot have any direct knowledge, but perceive only its action on ourselves; second, the states [of consciousness] in which we acknowledge the predominant manifestation of our own nature or which are determined by this nature; and third, the phenomena in which we feel that we are defined by something having a different kind of substantiality from ourselves, but not external to us, rather, so to speak, even more internal, more profound and central than we ourselves — phenomena in which we do not feel subordinate or constrained but, just the opposite, are elevated above ourselves and receive inner freedom. The phenomena [states of consciousness] of the first type relate to so-called external or physical experience, those of the second type to internal or psychic experience in the narrow sense of these terms, and those of the third type are mystical phenomena.

Empirical philosophy in all its phases attributes the meaning of objective reality only to the givens of external experience, rejecting or ignoring mystical experience; it acknowledges psychic phenomena only as secondary subjective variants of physical phenomena. The remaining systems of academic philosophy, completely acknowledging the independent reality of internal, or psychic, phenomena and their irreducibility to external experience, decisively reject the independence of mystical phenomena, considering them to be merely abnormal, unhealthy variants of psychic life. Concerning abnormality, in philosophy it would be advisable to be very careful with this word and never to forget its purely relative meaning. In the present case, if one sees mystical phenomena as being only abnormal psychic ones, then why can these same psychic phenomena be acknowledged as abnormal physical ones? On the other hand, there existed and still exist religious and philosophical systems, which the entire physical and psychic worlds acknowledge as abnormal variants of mystical existence, as breaking away from it. Apparently, all this is completely subjective and devoid of positive philosophical meaning. A more serious matter is the prevailing general tendency in modern science to attribute phenomena of one type to one of the others, and moreover, phenomena that are more profound and central to what is superficial or peripheral: to equate gods with a person, a person with an animal, and an animal with a machine. In other words, to extract a full existence that is rich in content and power from an existence that is barren, feeble, and empty. This tendency is completely necessary in the present stage of mental development, and consequently one can encounter it not only in science, but even where it would be difficult to imagine it; nevertheless, it must remain only a tendency, because its actual realization, the actual reduction of a plus to a minus, is logically impossible, since it contradicts the basic axiom *ex nihilo nihil*.[2] If, for example, the phenomena of organic life, which contain all the basic elements and forms of inorganic existence, also possess over and above that some sort of new content, certain characteristic features that specifically make them organic, then this new content evidently can no longer be taken from inorganic existence, in which it does not occur, and consequently the organism *as such* cannot be reduced to a mechanism. In the light of this, contemporary scholars simply ignore the particular, specific character of one or another class of phenomena, and at that point what is opened up to them is a complete free range for all sorts of reductions and deductions. By ignoring the personal life in an organism and self-consciousness in a person, it goes without saying, it does not cost anything to reduce them to a simple machine, but then this very method with all its results is absolutely worthless and can deceive only children or people with preconceived ideas. Nevertheless, this tendency of contemporary science, false in its exclusiveness, has in a certain sense not only a historical but also a general philosophical justification. It is correct, first, insofar as it affirms the essential unity and internal connection of *all* forms of existence, and its delusion lies only in the fact that it seeks this unity and this connection not in the general absolute center of every being, but in one of the spheres of this being, and moreover in the lowest and most superficial sphere. In other words, its delusion here has to do with the confusion of a peripheral unity with a central unity. Second, the aforementioned tendency is correct, even in affirming the *dependence* of the higher spheres of being on the lower ones, but it incorrectly relates this dependence to *existence* itself, supposing that the higher entities do not possess being in themselves and for themselves, but receive it only from the lower creatures, when in fact the dependence here relates only to the *manifestation*, i.e., to existence for an other.

We cannot, however, discuss this subject in more detail yet, and therefore return to the question of the reality of mystical phenomena. The acknowledgment of this reality, as of any other kind, can be based exclusively on experience. This experience is given in the entire history of humankind; we find it in all centuries and in all peoples — perhaps not in all people personally; in the question of the reality of known phenomena, however, the number of their *subjects* apparently does not matter. The quantitative point of view here would lead to astonishing conclusions. If most of humanity consisted of those born blind, light would be a hallucination and those with sight, visionaries. In the enormous mass of the inorganic world, living creatures are an insignificant minority, and among them a similar insignificant minority is made up of self-conscious creatures; those who do not negate life and spirit on this statistical basis should not reject mystical phenomena, either. All that is grand in our midst is an exception, and the scarcity of diamonds only increases their worth. Incidentally, I would never finish if I wanted to mention all the illogicalities in the current arguments against mysticism. Among these arguments, even the one typically used by thinking people, in presenting the evident (μετάβασις εἰς ἄλλο γένος),[3] is beneath any kind of criticism. It refers specifically to the affirmation of the *impossibility* of mystical phenomena a priori: they are impossible, consequently they do not exist. But a purely a priori question concerning the possibility, i.e., the conceivability, may relate only to concepts and judgments, but in no way to phenomena as such. By the term "phenomenon" one understands something that is experienced, empirically given, i.e., undergone by a subject, his actual condition. For this reason one can ask whether a certain phenomenon *exists* or not, whether it is *real* or not, i.e., experienced by a subject or not, and whether it possesses an actual condition or not; the question concerning possibility here, evidently, is irrelevant. "An impossible phenomenon," "an unthinkable fact" — this is simply nonsense, wooden iron. Of course, this is not the case from the point of view of Hegelianism, in which reality is subsumed under conceivability.

But in its exclusivity the Hegelian point of view has already been judged by the history of thought, and depends on it — this means to make *petitio principii*.[4] Concerning free theosophy, it is free first and foremost from preconceived ideas and arbitrary negations; it perceives in the same way the *reality* of all three main types of phenomena. However, it goes without saying that as a consequence of their characteristic features, for free theosophy they do not have the same *significance*, existing among themselves in a certain hierarchical subordination according to their relationship to a general, absolute center. Mystical phenomena, as the most central and profound, possess primary and fundamental importance; psychic phenomena follow them; and finally, as the most superficial and not independent, physical phenomena. The sphere of physical being, as an external, peripheral unity, and consequently ultimate realization of what is existent, and the psychic sphere, as an internal intermediary between the center and the periphery, are indisputably necessary for the fullness of absolute being. Through the acknowledgment of this necessity free theosophy avoids the sentimental poverty of one-sided mysticism, for which *Natur ist Sünde, Geist ist Teufel*,[5] and which, in not possessing any firm foundation for itself, externally circles around in its own subjective feeling; while genuine theosophical mysticism, in being based on the divine principle, strives to make it flow into all humans and natural things, not destroying, but integrating both spirit and matter.

Thus the material of genuine philosophy as integral knowledge is acquired through the sum total of phenomena, both mystical, and psychic and physical as well. But the cognition of all these phenomena in their immediate detail does not yet form any kind of philosophy — they must receive *the form* of universal, integral truth, must concentrate on universal ideas. This concentration of private, experienced kinds of knowledge, this collection of separate trajectories of experience in the focus of ideas, cannot be the fruit of abstraction, since in that case in philosophy there would be less content than in experience, and it would not have raison d'être[6] as an independent activity. To be sure, abstract concepts are necessary for philosophy, as for any kind of knowledge, but only as a means, as abbreviation marks, as outlines of experience — they relate to philosophy as plans and maps relate to actual locations and countries. But an abstract concept by its very definition cannot go further than that from which it is abstracted, cannot transform incidental and particular facts into indispensable, universal truths or ideas. If particular phenomena in and of themselves do not present to us universal truths or ideas, then the latter, while materially linked with phenomena, must formally be distinguished from them, must have their own existence that is independent of phenomena, and consequently, for a knowledge of them a specific form of cognitive activity is necessary, which we, along with many previous philosophers, call "mental contemplation" or "intuition" (*intellektuelle Anschauung*, intuition) and which constitutes the actual primary form of integral knowledge. In consequence of the material link of phenomena to ideas, the *mental contemplation* of the latter always presupposes a *sensory perception* of the former — neither the latter nor the former exist separately, and the distinction in all spheres of our knowledge is only quantitative or measured, depending on whether phenomenal experience or the contemplation of ideas is predominant. The third form of cognition, abstract thought, as noted, does not have any positive content, but nevertheless to it belongs a particular, albeit purely negative, significance as the boundary or transition between sensory perception and mental contemplation. All general, abstract definitions contain the negation of everything that enters into the scope of its phenomena in their particular, immediate individuality, and along with this the affirmation of them in some kind of new unity and new content, which, however, the abstract concept, remaining purely negative, does not provide in itself but only points out — every general concept is *the negation of a phenomenon and the indication of an idea.* Thus, for example: in the general conception of "person" is contained, first, the negation of a particular individuality, of this or that person taken separately, and second, the affirmation of all of them in a certain new, higher unity that embraces all of them but concomitantly has its own specific objectivity independent of them. However, a general conception of it evidently does not provide this very objectivity, this very content of higher unity, or this very positive idea of a person. Hence it is clear that abstract thought is a transitional state of the human mind when it is strong enough to free itself from the power of sensory perception and relate to it negatively, but is not yet able to grasp the idea in all the fullness and integrality of its real, objective being, to unite with it internally and essentially, or perhaps only to brush against its exterior, to skim over its external forms.

The fruit of such a relationship is not a living image or likeness of the existent idea, but only its shadow, designating its external boundaries and contours, but without the fullness of its forms, strengths, and colors. Hence it is easy to see that abstract thought deprived of any personal content must serve either as an *abbreviation of sensory perception* or as a *reflection of mental contemplation,* insofar as the general concepts that form it may be underscored either as an *outline of phenomena* or as *shadows of ideas* reinforced by words. As a consequence of the absence of the personal content in abstract concepts, they are often mistaken for ideas. This confusion is the basis, incidentally, for the famous dispute in scholasticism between the realists and the nominalists. Both sides were essentially correct. The nominalists, in emphasizing *universalia post rem,*[7] understood originally by *"universalia"* general concepts, and in this sense rightly demonstrated their lack of independence and secondary meaning as only *nomina* or *voces*. On the other hand, the realists, in emphasizing *universalia ante rem*,[8] had in mind genuine ideas and soundly demonstrated their primacy.

But since both sides poorly distinguished these two meanings of the word *universalia,* or at any rate did not define this distinction with sufficient precision, endless disputes had to arise between them.

The existence of ideal intuition in general, undoubtedly, is proved by the fact of artistic work. In actuality, those ideal images that are given substance by the artist in his creative works are neither, in the first place, a simple reproduction of observed phenomena in their private and incidental reality nor, in the second place, general concepts abstracted from this reality. Just as an observation, so an abstraction or generalization is necessary for the elaboration of artistic ideas, but not for their creation; otherwise, every observing and contemplating person, every scholar and thinker could be a genuine artist, which in reality is not the case. Everyone who is somewhat acquainted with the process of creative work knows well that creative ideas and images are not complex products of observation and reflection, but appear to the mind's eye in their internal totality. The work of the artist is concentrated only on their development and manifestation in material details. Everyone knows that abstract reasonableness and the slavish imitation of reality are to an equal degree deficiencies in an artistic work. Everyone knows that a genuine artistic image or type indisputably needs the internal combination of complete individuality with complete generality, or universality, and such a combination indeed composes the essential feature or attribute of the genuine mentally contemplated idea, as distinct from an abstract concept, to which belongs only the community, and from a particular phenomenon, to which belongs only individuality. Thus if the subject of art can be neither a particular phenomenon that is accessible to external observation nor a general concept that is produced by reflection, then this subject may be only an integral idea open to mental contemplation, or intuition.

But since the mental contemplation of ideas exists, the question arises: Must it be limited to art, or can it also serve as the basic form of genuine philosophy? If scholastic philosophy in its two manifestations, relying either on external observation or on abstract thought, avoids every kind of intuition and is closer to mathematics than to art, then philosophy as integral knowledge, the subject of which lies beyond the bounds both of observed phenomena and of abstractly conceived concepts, may be based only on mental contemplation as the primary form of genuine cognition, and in this respect represents an essential closeness with art. The fundamental difference between them is contained in the following: art has as its subject this or that idea considered separately, independently of its relationship to everything else, while philosophy has as its subject not this or that idea, but the entire cosmos of ideas, i.e., the general aggregate of ideas in their internal relationship or interaction, as an objective expression of the truly-existent. But since the ideal world in all its reality may be accessible only to endless or absolute cognition, philosophy must limit itself to well-known central ideas, leaving the ideal periphery to art, which reproduces it in its parts. But the more central, more profound, and more universal the idea, the less possible is its direct contemplation for a person in his present eccentric or peripheral condition; for this reason, philosophical intuition to a significant extent yields in brightness and intensity to artistic intuition, surpassing it [however] by its universality of content. Furthermore, since a real *connection* between ideas and the integrality of the ideal cosmos is determined by its absolute center, a spontaneous contemplation of this connection and integrality is accessible only to the gaze located in that center. For the human mind only a secondary, reflexive, purely logical cognition of transcendental relationships is possible, i.e., cognition of them in a general form, which, being the same for everything that exists, may be detached or abstracted from any kind of evidence at all. In other words, we may apprehend transcendental relationships only by analogy with the immanent ones; we may apprehend in the first ones only what they have in common with the last ones, and thus, although the fundamental ideal content of genuine philosophical cognition is necessarily gained only by mental contemplation of ideas, the organization of this content into a single whole or reproduction of the ideal cosmos is possible for our philosophy only by the most general and purely logical scheme. The constituent elements of philosophy are mentally contemplative ideas, and in this respect it is identical with art, but the general connection of these ideas is realized by abstract thought — philosophy itself as a system is a purely logical construction, and in this lies its distinctiveness.

However, presupposing authentic mental contemplation as the basic form of genuine cognition, we uncover a new question. Since mental contemplation or direct cognition of ideas is not the usual condition for a person, and along with this does not at all depend on his will, since not everyone and not at all times is given the food of the gods, the question arises: Which *active source* leads a person to the possibility of apprehending existent ideas? It is evident that we cannot, from out of ourselves a priori, obtain any kind of real knowledge about something else. If our actual cognition of external phenomena depends on the action on us of external beings or things, then similarly real cognition or the mental contemplation of transcendental ideas must depend on the internal action on us of ideal beings, or of transcendental ones. The fact of the matter is that neither phenomena nor ideas can exist in and of themselves, and likewise cannot be the purely subjective attributes of our being (since in that case there would not exist an originating attribute): both the one [phenomena] and the other [ideas], consequently, possess their own subjects, and the action of these subjects produces on us a sensory cognition of phenomena and similarly a mental contemplation of ideas. Empiricism, in striving for an objective knowledge of phenomena apart from the beings subject to them, comes to a subjective illusion; an abstracted idealism based on rationalism that emphasizes ideas in and of themselves, without ideal beings, it receives instead of real ideas only general, abstracted concepts that consequently turn out to be subjective thoughts. The objective reality of ideas and likewise of phenomena may be affirmed only upon the distinction of that which is existent (and those that are existent) in and of itself from its ideal and real forms: as manifestations of particular beings, both ideas and phenomena, so to speak, are *anchored* and become objective. The action on us of ideal beings that produces in us a mentally contemplative cognition (and creative work) of their ideal forms or ideas, is called *"inspiration."* This action leads us out of our usual natural center, elevates us to a higher sphere, thus producing ecstasy. So, generally speaking, the acting or directly determining principle of genuinely philosophical knowledge is inspiration. Without origins in the inspiration of intuition, in truth, no objective activity and no objective cognition would be possible; but there is a difference in degree, and for philosophy as integral knowledge feelings of intuition and inspiration evidently possess a much greater significance than, for example, for mathematics.

In summarizing what has been said, we find that free theosophy in general is knowledge that has as its subject the truly-existent in its objective manifestation, as its goal the internal union of a person with the truly-existent, and as its material the givens of human experience in all its aspects, to wit: first mystical, then internal or psychic, and finally external or physical. As its primary form, free theosophy possesses mental contemplation or the intuition of ideas, connected in the overall system by means of purely logical, or abstract, thought, and finally, as its active source, or generative cause — inspiration, i.e., the action of higher, ideal entities upon the human spirit.

Characterization of Integral Knowledge

Such is the type of cognition that defines free theosophy in general as a system of genuine philosophy. Insofar as here, from out of one mystical center, the proceeding synthesis embraces in its hierarchical, separable unity all the cognizable elements, which in other systems and currents of philosophy develop in their particularity and one-sidedness, this type of cognition in fairness may be called "integral knowledge." Outside of it are possible only these or isolated one-sided tendencies, or their mechanical juxtaposition, or fruitless eclecticism that attempts to describe the circumference without a center or radius. The real significance of integral knowledge, elevated to a system, like the real significance of anything at all, may be shown only in actuality, i.e., as a realization of this system. But there exist opinions, which in advance do not want to admit to such a realization, emphasizing the *impossibility* of integral knowledge. This latter first and foremost claims to be knowledge about the essence of things, about that which is rather than that which only seems to be; but precisely this is acknowledged as impossible from the point of view of *skepticism*. This skepticism appears in general current opinion, and likewise equally in the formulas of academic philosophy.

Concerning the first, popular skepticism, it can be reduced to the assertion that because of our mental limitations we cannot have any true knowledge about the essence of things, and consequently cannot have any central or integral knowledge: *in's Innre der Natur dringt kein erschaffner Geist*.[9] But how can we know that the human mind is limited? By eyewitnessing, or from experience, or a priori. Experience here can be either personal or historical. But personal experience in the present case, evidently, may have only what is personal and the application of it. For this reason the more reasonable among the popular skeptics, keeping silent about personal experience, cite directly from history: "Historical experience has proved that the human mind is capable neither of any true knowledge about the essence of things, nor of any real metaphysics."[a] So be it! But every kind of experience relates to a certain type of phenomena in a certain, given time, and in no way can have unconditionally a universal significance. Thus, being grounded in historical experience, we could, if you will, emphasize that the human mind in its past development and up

---

a. Here I use the word "metaphysics" in the sense in which it is usually accepted in popular skepticism, specifically in the meaning of every kind of cognition of the existence of things, of every kind of transcendental cognition.

to the present minute did not encounter success in the search for metaphysical truth. But since we definitely do not know what kind of relationship exists between the time humankind has already lived through and what it will experience in the future, the conclusion from lack of success in the past to absolute inability may in the given case turn out to be just as unfounded as if we, in seeing a three-month-old child, were to emphasize that it was completely unable to talk, because up to that time it could not utter a single word. Since we do not know anything at all about the relative age of humankind, we do not have the right to deny that its presupposed inability to grasp metaphysical knowledge may be of the same kind as the inability of a three-month-old child to talk. But since we must concede that in a certain phase of humankind's development, in some indefinite future time, it may be capable of metaphysical cognition, how can we be certain that this future has not already appeared at the present moment? Thus, on the basis of historical experience we cannot maintain decisively anything reliable concerning the abilities or lack thereof of the human mind with respect to metaphysics. Or, perhaps this inability, this limitation of the human mind, arises not from experience, but must be recognized as inherent to its very nature, in lying in its inner essence and therefore absolutely indispensable? But such an affirmation already presupposes that the essence of the human mind is known to us, since otherwise we could not know what was peculiar to it in its essence — it presupposes, it follows, a knowledge of some kind of essence, i.e., metaphysical knowledge. Thus, here the negation of any kind of metaphysics is based on a certain metaphysical knowledge, and the argument brings about its own destruction.

Turning now to a stricter academic skepticism, we can easily see that it must be presented in three forms, depending upon whether or not the object of cognition is taken as the point of departure, i.e., in the present case the truly-existent as an absolute principle, or cognizing subject, or the nature of knowledge itself in its reality. In all three forms, as will be shown now, skepticism argues on the basis of certain presupposed ideas, or *petitiones principii*, and thus emerges as nothing more than a prejudice.

The first kind of skeptical argument is reduced to the assertion that the presupposed subject of any kind of metaphysics is the *Ding an sich*, or the existent (thing) in itself, that it is something by its nature not cognizable, since we apparently may know only a phenomenon, i.e., that which appears to us, which exists relative to us and for us as an other, and not the existent (thing) alone in itself. This assertion is evidently based on the presupposition that the existent (thing) in itself, or *Ding an sich*, cannot be a phenomenon as well, i.e., exist for an other. Meanwhile, this is only a presupposition. To affirm the nonmanifestability and, consequently, unknowability of the truly-existent, it is necessary to have some sort of definite understanding of it, and if it is impossible to grasp its positive idea before attaining a genuine knowledge of it, i.e., before attaining a definite and complete metaphysical system, then in any case it is possible and necessary to give it preliminarily some kind of general, relative definition that characterizes it not in its own self, but only with respect to what we already know, what is given to us in our experience, i.e., with respect to genuine phenomenal being. And here we must define the truly-existent in two ways. First, we define it as that which *is not* genuine phenomenal being. This is self-evident. But this "is not" expresses not unconditional opposition, but only distinction or partial opposition (in the sense that we may say, for example, that an animal is not a plant). In reality, in distinguishing metaphysical essence from the given phenomenal being, we must nevertheless admit between them a certain necessary correspondence and say, secondly, that the truly-existent represents the absolute origin of all phenomenal being. This is because the very concept of the latter presupposes that it does not contain in itself its own authentic origin (since in that case it would be not a phenomenon, but an essence), and consequently has this authentic origin in something else, which already is not a phenomenon or manifestation, but the truly-existent. But if a metaphysical entity is defined as the absolute origin of all phenomena, then it no longer can be understood as what is existent in itself or for itself *exclusively* (Kant's *Ding an sich*), as something absolutely simple and undifferentiated — underlying it is already emphasized some sort of relationship to an other, and moreover a relationship that is specific and complex. This is because if we do not want to make judgments about empty abstract concepts, we must not conceive of a metaphysical entity as only the *general* origin of phenomenal being *in abstracto:* we must examine it as the *real* origin of *real* phenomena in all their endless diversity; in other words, the truly-existent must contain in itself the positive principle of all particular forms and properties of our real world, and it must possess to the superlative degree all its fullness and reality. Thus, according to the most general definition of a metaphysical entity, it cannot be merely a simple and undifferentiated *Ding an sich*, but as a real origin or positive principle of all phenomena, it must in a certain way contain in itself all the relative forms and realities of our real world, and in addition an indefinite multitude of other forms and realities (since our phenomenal world is not something that is finished: there constantly arise new phenomena, the real origin of which must lie in the metaphysical sphere). And if this is the case, then between the phenomenal world known to us and the metaphysical world as its authentic origin there must be a particular correspondence, on which is affirmed the possibility of metaphysical knowledge.

When people say that we must cognize only phenomena, and in no wise the existent in itself, they presuppose between the one and the other an unconditional separateness that does not allow any interaction. But precisely this presupposition is not only lacking in any kind of basis, but it is completely absurd. A phenomenon is a phenomenon of something, but of what can it be a phenomenon, if not of the existent in itself? This is because everything exists in itself, or in an other — the existent or the phenomenon. It is evident that we may in general know only that which is revealed or appears for us as an other, in a word, that which is a phenomenon — to be a phenomenon and to be known means one and the same thing — but precisely the extent to which a phenomenon is nothing other than a discovery, or cognizability, of the existent in itself, in knowing a phenomenon, we possess by the very same a certain knowledge of this existent, which reveals itself in a phenomenon. It is completely evident that our cognition cannot contain this existent either in its own authentic being or materially, as an image in a mirror does not materially contain in itself the reflected object, since in that case they would be identical and there would no longer be a reflection. However, as this image in a mirror nevertheless gives us a truthful representation of the object itself, insofar as it can be reflected, i.e., in its form, in the same way our cognition, even though it cannot embrace a metaphysical being in its internal reality or subjective content, nevertheless can and must be an adequate reflection of this being in its form, or subjective content, which indeed is nothing other than reflection or being for an other of that internal essence that is inaccessible in its own self. Thus the assertion that we cognize only phenomena, in the indicated meaning, is more than true — it is tautological and means only that we cognize what is knowable and that cognizability or the objective existence of an entity, its existence for an other, is not the same thing as its subjective existence in itself. The concept of "phenomenon" as a discovery or as what is perceptible to the eye presupposes two terms: the entity apparent and an other, for which and to which it appears, and it is evident that on the basis of their relationship to each other the phenomenon may be a more or less direct expression of what has appeared, but in any case it is a relationship, existence for an other.

These observations allow us to give a possibly accurate logical definition of that which is called "the existent in itself" *(an sich)* and "the phenomenon." By "phenomenon" I have in mind the cognizability of an entity, its objectivity or existence for an other; by "existent in itself or of itself" I have in mind the same entity, insofar as it does not relate to an other, i.e., in its own subjective reality. Directly from here emerges the correlation of these categories and complete impossibility to attribute one of them to metaphysical essence exclusively, and the other just as exclusively to the world of our real experience, thus separating these two areas and making one absolutely inaccessible for the other. It follows that the distinction between our ordinary cognition and metaphysical cognition may be only relative or graded. If our ordinary cognition could relate only to phenomena as such, excluding any kind of link with what has appeared, and metaphysical cognition were cognition of the existent in itself as such, i.e., immediately, excluding any kind of phenomenon or revelation, then between them there really could not be anything in common. But since the immediate cognition of the existent, i.e., its cognition besides its cognizability, or objectivity, is an apparent absurdity and since, on the other hand, in any cognition of a phenomenon we cognize more or less the appearing entity, since in the opposite case the phenomenon would exist in and of itself, which is likewise absurd, then it follows that every kind of real cognition, as physical, so also metaphysical, is, from a material standpoint, the cognition of the existent in its phenomena, and the difference may consist only in the sense that some phenomena represent a closer and more perfect revelation of the existent than others. If it is necessary to point out a definite distinction between physical and metaphysical cognition, we will say that the latter has in mind the existent in its immediate and integral revelation, while our physical knowledge is concerned only with the particular and secondary phenomena of the existent (the precise meaning of these terms will be completely clear to us only later).

The second kind of skeptical argument that issues from the cognizing subject can be reduced to the assertion that our mind as cognizing is subject to certain necessary forms and categories, from which it cannot come out, and consequently it can never attain cognition about the existent itself that is independent of those subjective forms and categories of our mind.

Here we again encounter a misunderstanding and a preconceived opinion. That all our external knowledge, everything that is given in our physical experience, and hence our entire physical world, is defined by the forms and categories of a cognizing subject — this is a great and irrefutable truth. That our space and time (no longer having in mind the categories of our reason) in its given reality belongs to the cognizing subject, and not to things outside it, is a truth just as indisputable as it is important, of which we will become convinced later — and the clear development of these truths constitutes the eternal merit of the idealism founded by Kant. However, that the indicated forms *by their very nature, ipso genere,* are subjective, i.e., that our space and time and the categories of our reason cannot have anything corresponding to them beyond the boundaries of our subject and his cognition — such an assertion not only has not been proved, but neither Kant nor his successors even attempted to prove it because of the obvious impossibility of doing it, while the opposite assumption is more than probable; that metaphysical substance is not defined by *our* actual space and *our* actual time is obvious; but whether or not it is subject to these or other forms *in general,* i.e., whether or not it contains in itself anything corresponding to them, is a completely different question; and we saw that the most general definition of metaphysical being demands the admission that it in a certain way possesses all the relative forms of our world. In any case, as soon as it is impossible to prove that forms of our cognition are subjective *unconditionally,* i.e., by its very nature, the general possibility of metaphysical cognition from the standpoint of the subject is allowed.

The third kind of skeptical argument affirms that since all the real content of our cognition can be reduced to our representations or to the states of our consciousness, while metaphysical essence cannot be our representations, then it follows that for us it is uncognizable. There cannot be any doubt that we can cognize only in our own representations or states of our consciousness; however, as shown in the preceding chapter, these representations of ours cannot exist in and of themselves — they presuppose besides their subject another defining objective cause and are themselves nothing other than only the cognizability of this cause. On the other hand, it is worth noting that since every phenomenon is the existence of a being for an other or the representation of this existence through an other, the assertion that metaphysical being cannot become a representation or a state of consciousness of an other is equivalent to the assertion that it in general cannot be manifested or become apparent, i.e., come into being for an other. But this, in the first place, contradicts the very definition of metaphysical being, and in the second place, since a phenomenon in general cannot be in and of itself, but the phenomenon of the existent is necessary, then to emphasize the lack of manifestation of the existent means simply to deny the very existence of phenomena, which already is completely absurd.

From the aforementioned it follows that the truly-existent is not an exclusive, simple, and undifferentiated substance, but rather possesses all the powers of real and complete being; that phenomena cannot be separated from the existent and that in them it is more or less cognized; that the subjective existence of our cognizing forms does not prevent them from corresponding to independent realities beyond the boundaries of the cognizing subject; and that if all the elements of our cognition are representations or images, then through them the existent is represented or depicted, and it follows that through them it may be cognized. All this leads to the notion that cognition about the truly-existent or about the existence of things both from the standpoint of the cognized object and from that of the cognizing subject, and also equally by the nature of cognition itself, must be acknowledged as possible, which was imperative to demonstrate.

Having eliminated the prejudices of skepticism and thus having shown the general possibility of integral knowledge in the capacity of the metaphysical knowledge of the essence of things, we return to the interrupted thread of our exegesis. By defining at the beginning of the present chapter subject, goal, material, form, and active source of cognition in free theosophy, we were not speaking *explicite* about organic logic, since in the indicated five relationships there is no essential distinction among the separate parts of free theosophy. Turning now to the specific characterization of organic logic, we must for a definition of it as such, i.e., in its logical character, first and foremost examine other existing forms of scientifically designed logic. In the most general definition logic *in genere* is the science or study of thought, and the typological distinctions depend on the perspective from which thought is derived and how it is understood. One can take thought exclusively as something given, as a subjective process, and describe its general methods without any kind of relationship to any sort of content whatsoever. Elementary logic, usually called "formal," relates to thought in such a way. It pays attention exclusively to the given general forms of the mental process in their abstractness (concepts, judgments, mental conclusions as such), while what is thought, i.e., any content of ideas, judgments, and mental conclusions, appears in it only *exempli gratia*.[10] This is the grammar of thought, and it can be only of a pedagogical significance. As a purely descriptive discipline, this logic does not have anything in common with philosophy, and therefore we need not dwell on it.

Philosophical logic is concerned not with the process of thought in its general subjective forms as given empirically, but rather with the objective character of this thought as cognizing. The question of cognition is, obviously, a question about the relationship of the cognizing to that which is cognized or, speaking more precisely, about the relationship of the subjective forms of our mind to the reality independent from them, which is cognized through them. Here we first and foremost encounter critical logic, which acknowledges these two fundamental factors of our cognition as unconditionally independent of each other, without any kind of internal necessary connection with each other. For Kant the cognitive categories of our mind possess an exclusively a priori character and are inherently only empty subjective forms deprived of any objective content or reality, whereas, on the other hand, the actual content of our knowledge, given in sensory perception, possesses an exclusively empirical character, deprived of any community and necessity. Genuine, objective cognition, which cannot amount to either an empty form or an accidental empirical fact, obviously must consist of a synthesis of these two elements, and must combine the reality of sensory perception with universal community and the necessity of the a priori form. But precisely such a synthesis is impossible from the point of view of critical logic, which emphasizes both factors of cognition in unconditional separateness and abstractness, not allowing anything in common between them. In reality, with such an unconditional opposition of the a priori and empirical element, it is impossible to allow anything of a third kind between them; consequently, the required connection must itself possess either a purely empirical or a purely a priori character, but in the first case it is deprived of universal community and necessity, and consequently cannot convey to cognition the character of objective *truth*, while in the second case it is only a subjective form, not being able to convey to cognition objective *reality*. Thus critical logic does not give us the possibility of cognition — it [cognition] is impossible due to the mutual independence of its two fundamental factors. And so, what remains is to allow a dependence between them. First, one can assert that the empirical content of our cognition depends on a priori forms. This assertion forms the logic of rationalism, subsequently developed by Hegel.

Hegel asserts, first, that every given reality is unconditionally defined by logical categories, and second, that these categories themselves are the dialectical self-development of the ideas as such or of the pure idea in and of itself. But "idea" in and of itself, without definite content, is an empty word, and the self-development of such an idea would represent constant creative work out of nothing. As a result, the logic of Hegel, with all the profound formal truthfulness of its particular deductions and transitions, in its totality devoid of any real meaning, any real content, constitutes thought in which nothing is pondered. If we make the opposite supposition and allow that forms of our cognition are unconditionally determined by empirical content, that all our knowledge is only a generalization of the givens of experience, then of course we will win reality but in the process lose the general and necessary character of cognition. In actuality, based on this assumption, the logic of empiricism consistently approaches the negation of the universality and necessity even of mathematical axioms. Thus, neither the logic of rationalism nor the logic of empiricism liberates us from the dilemma arrived at by critical logic: either empty logical forms without any real content, or incidental empirical givens without any objective truthfulness. And meanwhile, for academic philosophy, which allows only two factors of our cognition, there remains no other possible way out. Evidently in reality, since these two factors of cognition are allowed, either they are independent of each other, as critical logic acknowledges, or the empirical factor is determined by the logical one, according to the logic of rationalism, or finally, the logical factor depends on the empirical, as the logic of empiricism acknowledges. *Kritik der reinen Vernunft* [*Critique of Pure Reason*] of Kant, *Die Wissenschaft der Logik* [*The Science of Logic*] of Hegel, and *The System of Logic*[11] of Mill — here are three canonical books, among which academic philosophy must choose in the area of logic.

Thus, if the two commonly accepted factors of our cognition, regardless of which mutual relationship we put them in, cannot give to this cognition the combined character of objective truthfulness and reality, it is necessary either to accept the conclusions of consistent skepticism or, admitting the possibility of objectively truthful and real cognition, to acknowledge the inadequacy of those two factors in and of themselves and indicate a third, which communicates to our cognition its genuine significance.

Only that knowledge satisfies the requirements of our minds; only to that knowledge do we give the predicate of "truthfulness," which is the kind that contains a reality of content and reasonableness of form, the empirical element and purely logical element connected with each other not accidentally but by an internal organic bond. This bond, not consisting of both of these elements in and of themselves (since out of empirical content of our cognition in and of itself in no wise flows its logicalness, and out of the logical form of cognition in no wise flows its reality), presupposes a third principle, free from the one-sided opposition of two elements and in which they find their unity as two separate sides of this single principle. The empirical element and the purely logical one are two possible *modes of being,* the real and the ideal; the third absolute principle is defined neither by the one nor by the other mode of being, and consequently, in general is not defined as *being,* but as the positive origin of being, or *that which is existent.* This distinction of the existent from being is of an important, decisive significance not only for logic, but also for an entire worldview, and for this reason we must focus on it.

The given subject of every kind of philosophy is the real world, both the external and the internal. But as the given of philosophy proper, this world may be not in its particular forms, phenomena, and empirical laws (in this sense it is a given only of positive science), but in its commonness. If particular phenomena and laws are, as indisputable as this may be, distinct modes of being, their commonness is being itself. Everything that exists shares this commonness, specifically that it is, i.e., being. From here it is easy to assume that philosophy studies being, that it must answer the question of what constitutes being. And in reality, various philosophical systems answer this question; thus, naturalistic empiricism emphasizes, first, that being is matter, and later in analyzing this notion finds that matter amounts to sensation, and that consequently being is sensation; rationalistic idealism in its consistent development arrives at the definition of being as thought. Both of these philosophical currents, issuing from the opposition of objective and subjective being, reconcile them in this manner, the one in sensation, the other in thought: both are *being in general,* the identity of the subjective and the objective. But this reconciliation is completely illusory, consisting of the destruction of both reconciled terms. In reality thought *in general* and sensation *in general,* i.e., in which no one thinks anything or senses anything, are empty words, and consequently the empty word is also being *in general.* "Being" has two completely different meanings, and if one strays from this distinction, any definite meaning is lost, only the word remains. When I say "I am" or "this person is" — and subsequently when I say "this thought is," "this sensation is" — I am using the verb "to be" in a completely different sense. In the first case I am applying the predicate of being to a certain subject, while in the second to the predicate of the subject; in other words, I emphasize in the first case being as a real attribute of the subject, that it indeed exists in actuality, while in the second case I emphasize being only as a grammatical predicate of a real predicate that may possess only a grammatical meaning and not correspond to anything real. In actuality, this thought of mine and this sensation of mine are nothing other than certain modes of being of my subject, some form of my being, and when I say "I am," by "am," in distinction from "I," I have in mind specifically all the real modes of my being — thoughts, sensations, desires, etc. However, concerning these modes, whether taken separately or in and of themselves, I no longer can logically state that they *are*, similarly to when I say that "I am," since they are only in me as in a subject, when I am in them as in predicates, i.e., in the reverse manner. Therefore, when I say "this thought is" or "this sensation is," only grammatically are "thought" and "sensation" subjects with the predicate of being; logically they in no wise can be subjects, and consequently, being in no wise can be their predicate, so these assertions, "my thought is" and "my sensation is," mean only "I think," "I feel"; and in general "thought is," "feeling is" mean "someone thinks," "someone feels," or "there exists someone who thinks," "there exists someone who feels"; and finally, "being is" means that there is "someone who is existent." Consequently, in general such assertions in an absolute form are false. It is impossible to say simply and unconditionally: "thought is," "will is," "being is," because thought, will, and being are only there to the extent that there is someone who thinks, someone who wills, and someone who is existent. And all fundamental errors of academic philosophy amount to the hypostatization of predicates, and moreover, one of the directions of that philosophy takes predicates that are general and abstract, while the other direction takes predicates that are particular and empirical; to avoid these errors it is incumbent on us to acknowledge first and foremost that the real subject of philosophy is that which is existent in its predicates, and definitely not these predicates in and of themselves. Only then will our cognition correspond with that which is in reality, and not be empty thinking in which nothing is thought.

Thus, that absolute first principle, which only may make our cognition genuine and which is affirmed as the principle of our organic logic, first and foremost is defined as that which is existent, and not as being. This absolute principle, in its own characterizations inherent to itself, which constitute the necessary *prius* of our being, and similarly of our cognition, and consequently which represent the necessary condition of the unity of the one and the other, i.e., for truth — this principle, I say, in its internally inherent attributes, composes the entire content of organic logic. Since all its own attributes are internally necessary, they must logically flow out of its conception itself, and consequently we must first and foremost in the most precise manner possible define in general the concept of the existent as the absolute first principle.

If the general conception of some kind of particular entity defines it in relation to some kind of particular being as its constant predicate, then the general idea of the existent itself (the entity as such) must define it in relation to every kind of being or to being itself, because every kind of being is in the same way its predicate. And here we again must say that the *existent is not being,* i.e., that it itself cannot be the predicate of anything else. In actuality, it is the origin of all of being; if it itself had been being, we would possess some sort of being above all being, which is absurd. Thus, the origin of all being cannot itself be being. But it similarly cannot be designated as nonbeing; by "nonbeing" is usually implied unconditional absence, the deprivation of being. However, to the existent as the absolute first principle *belongs* every kind of being, and it follows that to it in no wise can be attributed only nonbeing in a negative sense. Thus, if that which is existent is neither being nor nonbeing, then it is *endowed with being* or *possesses being.* If to be deprived of something is powerlessness, or lack of might in relation to it, then the commanding of something is *might* or *power* over it, or its *positive potential.* That the existent represents the power of being is evident already, because it presupposes or produces being, i.e., manifests itself; since, in manifesting itself in being, it *does not cease as that which is existent* — it cannot exhaust itself or cross over without any remaining trace into its being, since then, with the disappearance of the existent as the producer or actor, being, too, as the act produced by it would have disappeared — it always remains a positive force, or might, of being, hence this is its own constant attribute. But precisely as a consequence of its not migrating wholly into being — which, it follows, inherently it is not tied to being, is free from it — we cannot, if we want to be completely accurate, even say that it — this absolute first principle — *is* the force of being, since such a definition would link it inextricably with being, which in reality is not there; we may only say that it *is endowed with* the force of being or possesses it.

Thus, *the existent as such or the absolute first principle is that which contains in itself the positive force of being,* and since the possessor is higher-ranking or more superior than that which is possessed, the absolute first principle more accurately must be called *"the superexistent"* or even *"the superpowerful."*

It is evident that this first principle in and of itself is entirely solitary; it may represent neither particular multiplicity nor abstract universality, because both presuppose a relationship and every relationship is a specific form of being and consequently does not enter into the existent as that which is not being.

Every defined being presupposes a relationship to an other (since a definition requires an other as that which is defined), and every quality is a sensation, i.e., the interaction or relationship between the two entities; in other words: being is the manifestation of the existent, or its relationship to an other.[b] In this manner, every kind of being is relatively, unconditionally only the existent. But this relationship or interaction between entities, this being of theirs for each other, is none other than cognition. In reality, every defined being, as we said, is sensation, but sensation is none other than the fundamental elementary form of cognition, and therefore every kind of being is a form of cognition. For this reason, you see, cognition is relative by necessity, by its very nature, and not accidentally. That which is cognized, the same as the cognizing, can no longer be called "being" — they are existents or entities, the relationships among which constitute being, or representation, or cognition.

The absolute first principle in and of itself as an unconditional unit, never being able by itself to become many but possessing all of multiplicity, cannot, as was shown, comprise the content (or be the matter) of cognition, since all material content of cognition is being (it then is not being). Does it follow from here that this first principle is uncognizable? This depends on the meaning of the expression "to be cognizable." If by this expression one understands *"to comprise the content of cognition itself,"* its matter, or directly to be subject to cognition, then evidently it does not. If

---

b. It is obvious that real being = phenomenon. Every type of real being is a phenomenon, and besides the phenomenon there is no real being. However, from this statement it does not follow that phenomenon is everything. This would follow only in the case that being were everything. But besides being there is the existent, without which being itself would be impossible, as a phenomenon would be impossible without that which was manifesting itself. The existent is that which manifests itself, while being is the phenomenon.

by the cognized one understands the existent object of cognition in and of itself, then not only is the absolute first principle cognizable, but it alone is only cognizable in its own sense, since it alone is authentically the existent. Thus the absolute first principle is unconditionally uncognizable, insofar as it can never become the material content itself of cognition, i.e., being, can never as such migrate into being, change into an object; along with this and by the very same token the absolute first principle is unconditionally and exclusively cognizable, insofar as it alone is the existent subject of cognition (since everything else is its manifestation), insofar as every kind of cognition of the predicate or being relates to the existent first principle as the subject of this predicate.

We cognize the truly-existent in everything we know; but we could not distinguish it from the personally cognized, from its ability to become manifest, if it had not been given to us yet in some other way, in and of itself. It cannot be given to us inherently in cognition — this would be a contradiction — but being the sole truly-existent, i.e., the substance of everything, it is also the primary substance of us ourselves, and thus it may and must be given to us not only from without, in its reflected manifestations forming our objective cognition, but also from within us, as our own foundation. The grand thought lying at the basis of any truth consists of the acknowledgment that in essence everything that is, is *one whole,* and that this whole does not represent some sort of existence or being but is deeper and higher than every kind of being; thus in general all being is only the surface, under which is concealed that which is truly existent as an absolute unity, and this unity comprises as well our own inner essence — in elevating ourselves above everything in daily life and existence, we directly experience this absolute substance, because at this point we become it. This absolute singularity is the first positive characteristic of the absolute first principle, and it is acknowledged by all, at least to some extent, profound metaphysical systems, both religious and philosophical, but it especially appears, as we know, in the speculative religions of the East. The contemplative East cognized that which is truly existent only in its first attribute of absolute singularity, excluding everything else, and since a religious person always wants to become like his deity and through this process unite with it, the constant striving of Eastern religions compels a person to turn his attention away from all multiplicity, all forms, and resultantly all of being. But the absolute superexistent is along with this the origin of all of being: as the sole superexistent — the origin of multiplicity, and as the integral superexistent — the origin of the particular, free from all forms, producing all of them. The absolute first principle is not only ἕν — it is ἕν καὶ πᾶν.¹² For this reason, those who want to know it only as the one who is exclusively solitary know only a detached, lifeless part of it, and their religion, both in theory and in practice, remains uncompleted, exclusive, barren, and lifeless, which we see in the East. On the other hand, the constant striving of the West is to sacrifice the absolute inner unity of the multiplicity of forms and individual features, so that its people cannot even understand unity otherwise than as only external order founded on traditional authority (be it the pope or the Bible) or on the formal power of the law (be it a constitutional charter or *suffrage universel*)¹² — such is the character of Western religion and the church, of Western philosophy and government, of Western science and society. Genuine universal religion, genuine philosophy, and genuine community must internally combine both of these impulses, having liberated themselves from their exclusivity, must cognize and realize on earth an authentic ἕν καὶ πᾶν.

What we have defined as the existent or superexistent as the absolute principle of every kind of being represents the first supreme principle of organic logic, and since this logic is the first fundamental component in the philosophical system of integral knowledge, this principle is unconditionally the first principle of our entire philosophy. The acknowledgment of this principle in and of itself is based on the recognition of the reality of our empirical being and our reason. In actuality, since being is a given, there necessarily is an existent; since a phenomenon is a given, there necessarily is that which has manifested itself; and since what is relative and derivative is a given, there necessarily is an absolute and a first principle. That which is relative exists without a doubt — of this we are absolutely certain; but in the very concept of relativity and finality is contained the presupposition of the absolute and the endless, from which final and relative things receive their reality. As a consequence, if we acknowledge the reality of these latter things, then out of logical necessity we must also acknowledge the reality of their absolute principle in and of itself. It goes without saying that this conclusion has force only in the event that we are convinced of the reliability of logic or reasonable thinking that compels us from relative being by its very concept to define the existent as an absolute first principle. But on what basis can we be convinced of the truthfulness of reasonable thinking? It is evident that logical arguments are not applicable where the matter concerns the reliability of logic itself; consequently, only an absolute certainty may again be the basis here. Thus the conviction in the reality of the absolute first principle in and of itself is based in general on two acts of absolute certainty: first, the certainty of the reality of finite, empirically given being, and second, the certainty of the truth of logical thought or reason. It is easy to see from here that psychologically or subjectively, i.e., *for us*, the certainty of the absolute first principle depends on the absolute certainty of empirical being and our reason; logically or objectively, i.e., in the essence of the matter itself, on the contrary, the certainty of empirical being and our reason as relative concepts depends on the certainty of an absolute existent and similarly on their unconditional origin, without which our reason could not be truthful, while empirical being could not be real; for this reason those views that ignore or negate the absolute first principle in its particular reality lead, as we have already seen, to a negation of reality and empirical being and our reasonable thinking, i.e., to unconditional skepticism.

At this point we can more clearly define the relationship of organic logic to other kinds of logic. All of them pose the question of the truthfulness and reality of our cognition, but in the light of this, academic logic in all its forms seeks to explain our cognition immanently, i.e., out of it itself, which is completely impossible, since our cognition possesses the indisputable qualities of relativity, conditionality, and derivativeness, and does not contain its origin in its own self. Therefore, all explanations of academic logic lead to negative results. The logic of criticism, in breaking down our cognition and arriving at two final indivisible elements — empirical being as matter and a priori reason as form — leaves open the question of the internal relationship of these two elements, whereas in this relationship lies the entire essence of the matter; when the logic of rationalism and the logic of empiricism attempt to resolve this dualism by the negation of one of the elements and the reduction of it to the other, as a consequence of their necessary correlation the destruction of one leads to the destruction of the other, and the result is pure nothing. Academic logic breaks down the organism of our cognition into its component parts or reduces all the parts to one, taken separately, which apparently is the negation of the organism itself; therefore, academic logic in all its forms deserves the appellation "mechanical." True logic, in acknowledging the nonindependence of the separate elements of our cognition (as the parts of an organism, taken separately, are nonindependent) and the relativity of our entire cognizing sphere, refers to the absolute first principle as the gen-

Characterization of Integral Knowledge

uine center, as a consequence of which the periphery of our cognition becomes closed, its separate parts and elements receive unity and spiritual connection, and it wholly appears as a genuine organism, as a consequence of which such logic in all fairness must be called "organic." This logic is based on the following indisputable deduction: if an area of our given cognition is relative, i.e., presupposes some absolute principle underlying itself, then only from this principle may it be explained — it must begin from it. In remaining on the periphery of our actual being and cognition, we apparently are not in a state to understand and explain whatever might present itself, since this very periphery requires an explanation; we must consequently either reject genuine cognition or transfer our mental center to that transcendental sphere where the truly existent shines with its own light, since for the truthfulness of cognition evidently it is necessary for the center of what is cognizing in either way to correspond with the center of what is cognized. If the task of philosophy is to explain everything that exists, then to resolve this task, remaining in the immanent sphere of actual human cognition, is just as impossible as giving a truthful explanation of the solar system by accepting our earth as the focus. However, the objection is usually expressed: In what manner can a person, himself a relative entity, step out of the sphere of his given reality and transcend into the absolute? Who proved that a person is that which academic philosophy takes him to be? That a person is unconditionally bounded by the world of apparent phenomena and the relative categories of his reason — this is, after all, only a *petitio principii,* a preconceived idea. And against this preconceived idea we on our part have the right to affirm that a person himself represents the highest revelation of the truly-existent, that all the roots of his own being lie in the transcendental sphere and that, as a consequence, he is not at all bound by those chains that academic philosophy wants to lay on him. However, we do not need arbitrary assertions. The absolute first principle or the truly-existent is the unconditionally necessary, utmost concept of our very reason, and without it, as we have seen, even our immanent cognition collapses. We imagine a choice not between transcendent and immanent kinds of cognition, but between transcendent cognition and the negation of any kind of cognition. Either the absolutely-existent as a principle, or the pure zero of unconditional skepticism — this is the dilemma for every consistent thinker, and in choosing the first, we stand only on the soil of the most sober reasoning.

The general conception of the absolute first principle, as affirmed by our abstract thought, has a negative character, i.e., in it is properly manifested *that it does not exist*, rather than *that it exists*. The positive content of this principle, its *central idea*, is given only to mental contemplation or intuition. The ability to have such intuition is a real property of the human spirit, and only in it is contained the foundation of genuine theosophy. But since the content of the absolute is given to us in ideal intuition, it can and must be confirmed by the reflection of our reason and organized into a logical system, i.e., the general logical necessity of this content must be demonstrated; it must be shown that all definitions constituting this content logically flow out of the very concept of the absolute first principle or that which is existent. These particular definitions of the existent, logically flowing out of its conception, form its inner cognizability or manifestability — its λόγος — and the science that studies them thoroughly is called "logic." This λόγος as containing the inner particular characteristics of the existent represents the absolute *prius* of every kind of being and cognition, or the absolutely necessary conditions for the very possibility of every kind of being and cognition, and from this perspective logic is defined as the science of the necessary conditions of cognition, or of its possibilities.

Since organic logic, having as its *point of departure* the concept (λόγος) of the absolute first principle or that which is existent, must from this very concept logically draw out all the essential characteristics of the existent in and of itself, then the *method* of this science may be only pure dialectical thinking, i.e., thinking that develops from the inside that is not dependent at all on incidental external elements. (The internal content of this thinking or its real objects are given, as noted, through ideal intuition.)

Dialectics is one of three fundamental philosophical methods; the two others are *analysis* and *synthesis*. Since I use these terms in a somewhat different connotation than is usually attached to them, I must provide a general definition of them here. By "dialectics" I have in mind the kind of thinking that from a general principle in the form of a concept produces its concrete content; since this content evidently must already be contained in the general principle (since otherwise thought would be creative work from out of nothing), but be contained only potentially, the act of dialectical thinking consists precisely of the transference of this potential content into actuality: the primary concept emerges as some kind of kernel or seed, continuously developing into an ideal organism.

By "analysis" I have in mind the kind of thinking that, given concrete being as a fact, can be traced back to its first general principles.

Characterization of Integral Knowledge

By "synthesis" I have in mind the kind of thinking that, in issuing from two different spheres of concrete being through the definition of their internal relationships, leads to their higher unity.

Among these three, dialectics is for the most part the method of organic logic, analysis — of organic metaphysics — and synthesis — of organic ethics. We will say more about the two latter methods in due course, but at this point let us say yet a few more words about the dialectical method.

Dialectics as a specific type of philosophical thinking appears initially in the Eleatic School, and after that in Gorgy. Here it has a purely negative character, serves only as a means of proof or refutation, and moreover is deprived of any systematization. Thus, Gorgy, in inferring from well-known general concepts (being, cognition) their concrete definitions and indicating the contradiction of these definitions, drew the conclusion of the unsoundness of the most general concept. In this way in his book *About Nature* he investigated three states: (1) that nothing exists; (2) that if something exists, it is not cognizable; and (3) that if something exists and is cognizable, it cannot be expressed. Plato introduced the idea of genuine dialectics as pure thought developing from the inside, but he did not realize it. This is even less the case with Aristotle, although in both of them we find rich material for our logic. We encounter in Hegel the first real application of dialectics as a mental process, leading the entire system of definitions out of a single general concept. For this reason we must indicate the relationship of his rationalistic dialectics to our own (which we in contrast will call "positive") and the essential differences between them.

First, Hegel identifies the immanent dialectics of our thought with the transcendental logos of that which is existent itself (not only in essence or in objective content, but also in existence) or, properly, completely negates this last, so for it our dialectical thought is an absolute creative process. Such a negation of the particular transcendental reality of the existent leads, as has been indicated, to absolute skepticism and absurdity. Positive dialectics identifies itself (our pure thought) with the logos of that which is existent only in *general essence* or *formally,* and not in *existence* or *materially;* it acknowledges that the logical content of our pure thought is identical to the logical content of that which is existent, in other words, that the same (more precisely, exactly the same) definitions we dialectically consider also belong to the existent, but completely independently (in existence or reality) of our thought. And not only do these definitions belong to the existent in and of itself in its own reality as its ideas, but even for us these definitions are accessible in their living reality far before any reflection and any type of dialectics, specifically in ideal mental contemplation; our dialectics are only a coherent reproduction of these ideas in their general logical schemes. Since insofar as that which is existent in its logical form is the defining principle of our abstract reflection as well (as the form of the body determines the form of the shadow), insofar as its characteristics become existent for our abstract thoughts or general concepts; insofar as, in other words, our reason is a reflected manifestation of the existent specifically in its general logical definitions, to that extent we may have as well those things that correspond to it, which are adequate for these definitions or concepts. According to Hegel, our dialectical thought is our own consciousness of that which is existent or its consciousness of its own self, and moreover, outside of this consciousness the existent does not exist at all. A positive dialectics is affirmed only as our consciousness of the absolute, not possessing realistically any direct connection with its consciousness of itself.

Second, Hegel takes as his point of departure all dialectical development, takes as his logical subject or basis not the concept of that which is existent, but the concept of being. But the concept of being in and of itself not only does not contain anything, but also in and of itself cannot have any thought, transforming immediately into the concept of *"nothing."* In positive dialectics the logical subject is the concept of that which is existent; in Hegel the concept itself in general as such, i.e., the concept as pure being, without any content, without what is thought and without that which is thinking, is a dual equivalence of the concept with being and of being with nothing. It is evident that the task of developing everything out of this nothing in and of itself, i.e., by its *content*, may be only a dialectical delusion, although its resolution could contribute and indeed did contribute for Hegel to the rich development of the dialectical *form*.

Third, since for Hegel that which is existent amounts without any remainder to being, and being without any remainder amounts to dialectical thought, this thought must exhaust all of philosophy by means of itself, and the logic based on it must be the only philosophical science; and if nevertheless Hegel allowed even over and above this a philosophy of spirit, it was only a concession to the general meaning or inconsistency, which is already proved by the means by which he makes a transition from logic to nature philosophy: as already noted long ago in Germany as well, this is nothing other than a logical *salto mortale*. From our point of view, by which we acknowledge the thought only by means of one of the forms or aspects of the manifestation of the existent, dialectics cannot encompass by means of itself all of philosophical cognition, and the logic based on it cannot represent all of philosophy: it is only the first, the most general and abstract component of it, its backbone, which receives the body, life, and movement only in the subsequent components of the philosophical system — metaphysics and ethics.

PART IV

Principles of Organic Logic (Continuation): Concept of the Absolute: Basic Definitions according to the Categories of the Existent, Essence, and Being

Integral knowledge by its definition cannot have an exclusively theoretical character: it must answer to all the requirements of the human spirit, must satisfy in its sphere all the highest aspirations of a person. To separate the theoretical or cognitive element from the moral or practical element, and the artistic and aesthetic element, would be possible only in those instances when the human spirit were broken down into several independent entities, one of which would be only will, another only reason, and the third only feeling. But since this does not exist and cannot be, since it is always necessary for the object of our cognition to be along with this the object of our will and feeling, purely theoretical, abstract scientific knowledge always was and will be a useless invention, a subjective phantom. Let people not point to the so-called exact sciences — mathematics and natural science — as pure knowledge not having any direct relationship to will and feeling. Precisely as a consequence of this, these forms of knowledge in and of themselves, in their separateness, do not have any significance even from the theoretical standpoint, do not satisfy even the cognitive requirements of a person, do not constitute truth. If in answer to the eternal question "what is truth?" someone were to answer, truth is that the sum of the angles of a triangle is equivalent to the two straight ones, or that the combination of hydrogen and oxygen creates water — would this not be a bad joke? The theoretical question concerning truth relates apparently not to particular forms and relationships of phenomena, but to the universal unconditional meaning or reason (Λόγος) of an existing being, and therefore the particular sciences and forms of cognition possess the meaning of truth not inherently, but only in their relationship to this Logos, i.e., as organic components of a common, integral truth; in their separateness they are either a simple amusement satisfying personal tastes[a] or an auxiliary means for the satisfaction of the material requirements of civilized daily life as one of the weapons of industry. Thus here as well these sciences nevertheless are linked with will and feeling: not with spiritual moral will, but with material lust and whims, and not with higher artistic feeling, but with lower sensations. Our science serves either God or Mammon, but it unavoidably must serve something: it cannot be absolutely independent.

It is not difficult to see that if a pure, absolutely independent knowledge is impossible, then also impossible is a pure, absolutely independent morality, i.e., free from every cognitive and aesthetic element (Kant's practical reason), and equally impossible is exceptional art, i.e., art completely independent from theoretical and moral elements.

Thus, the theoretical sphere of thought and cognition, the practical sphere of will and activity, and the aesthetic sphere of feeling and creative work differ from each other not in their constitutive elements, which in all of them are one and the same, but only in the comparative degree of predominance of one or another element in one or another sphere; the exclusive self-affirmation of these elements in their separateness always remained only a striving without any actual realization.

If in this manner truth, constituting the content of genuine philosophy, must be situated in a necessary relationship to will and feeling, answering to their higher requirements, then evidently the point of departure of this philosophy — that which is absolutely existent — cannot be defined only by mental activity alone, since will and feeling are likewise necessary. And really, that which is absolutely existent is required not only by our reason as a logically necessary assumption of every kind of particular truth (i.e., of every clear and precise concept, of every faithful judgment and every correct conclusion) — the absolutely-existent is likewise required by will as a necessary assumption of every kind of moral activity, as an absolute goal; finally, it is required likewise by feeling as a necessary assumption of every kind of enjoyment, as that absolute and eternal beauty, which by and through itself alone may cover the visible disharmony of sensual phenomena "and resolve by a solemn chord the tormented discord of their voices."

    a. The German naturalist Heckel compares scholars studying exclusively the accumulation of empirical material with those enthusiasts who collect sets of postal stamps.

Concept of the Absolute

The ideal content of the absolute principle according to these three relationships apparently may be revealed only by all of philosophy. Now we must first and foremost turn our attention to its logical meaning, especially since the term "the absolute" is used very often and misused in various philosophical studies.

According to the sense of the word, "absolute" *(absolutum,* from *absolvere)* means, first, *not connected* to anything, *liberated,* and second, *completed, finished, full, whole.* Thus, already in a verbal connotation are contained two characteristics of the absolute: in the first it is defined by itself, in its separateness or estrangement from everything else and, as a consequence, *negatively* with respect to this everything else, i.e., to everything particular, finite, plural — it is defined as free from *everything,* as absolutely *united;* in the second meaning it is defined *positively* with respect to the other, as possessing everything, not being capable of having anything outside of itself (since in the reverse case it would not be completed and whole). Both meanings together define the absolute as ἓν καὶ πᾶν. It is apparent, moreover, that both meanings necessarily are combined in the absolutely-existent, since they presuppose each other, the one inconceivable without the other, being only two inseparable sides of one and the same characteristic. In actuality, to be free from everything it is necessary to possess might and power over everything, i.e., to be everything in positive potential or to be *the force of everything;* on the other hand, it is possible to be everything only by not being anything exclusively or in isolation, i.e., being free from everything or not connected to anything.

Thus it is easy to see the intimate interrelationship or correspondence between the concept of the absolute and the concept of the existent, because the existent as well, as we have seen in the previous chapter, represents with respect to being the same two sides, inseparable from each other, connected, defining themselves jointly both as free from any kind of being and as the positive principle of being.

From what has been said it is likewise clear that our understanding of the absolutely-existent, constituting the point of departure of the first theosophical science and, consequently, lying at the basis of the entire system of integral knowledge, *toto coelo,*[1] differs from the "absolute" of rationalist philosophy. In the latter the absolute is understood only in one of two meanings discernible to us, and since one receives its entire content from the other, it follows that here by "the absolute" exactly nothing is borne in mind; i.e., it is the same kind of empty word, as indeed are all the other fundamental concepts of this philosophy — being, nothingness, etc. In being inherently an empty word, this absolute is filled with content and becomes real only *genetically*, by means of self-development in the dialectical process. The genuine absolute necessarily and eternally contains in itself all of being and all realities, always remaining, in this manner, higher than this being and this reality. In it there cannot be any kind of process. Every process, every development, every dialectical transition from general, abstract, and potential definitions to definitions that are more concrete and valid belong only to us, to our thought, which gradually, in a temporal succession, seeks to attain that content, which in the absolute itself exists as a single eternal act.

The absolutely-existent, as indicated, is necessary *for us*, i.e., is required by our reason, our feeling, and our will. But does its own objective reality follow from this, and if it does not follow from it (as is apparent), then on what basis may we confirm this personal reality of the absolute? It is evident that the reality of something else may have in us only a passive basis, i.e., we cannot confirm ourselves from ourselves, but may only apprehend it as an action of this other upon us. And undoubtedly, in all human entities what lies deeper than any definite feeling, idea, or will is the direct sensation of absolute reality, in which the action of the absolute is apprehended by us directly, in which we, so to speak, come into contact with the self-existent. This sensation, not connected with any definite content, but subject to every kind of content, in and of itself is the same in everyone, and only when we want to connect it with some kind of exclusive expression (positive or negative — it does not matter), want to translate it into the confining language of definite feeling, idea, and will, then inevitably will all possible disagreements and arguments appear. For this reason, here, if anywhere, it makes sense to hold on, not to words or names, but to direct sensation or feeling.

> And if in feeling you are blessed completely,
> Call it as you wish — I don't know
> Its name. Feeling is everything, but a name
> Is only one sound or smoke that surrounds
> The deathless heat of heavenly fire.[2]

Every kind of cognition holds on to the uncognizable, all kinds of words refer to what is unspoken, and every kind of reality amounts to the one we possess in our own selves in unmediated feeling.

Concept of the Absolute

Through this unmediated feeling we are given *the unity in everything*, but it is necessary likewise to cognize *everything in the unity*. The absolute is not only reality, not only existence, it is likewise full of *content*, and therefore it is impossible to limit oneself to a single affirmation of its proper reality on the basis of unmediated sensation; it is necessary to cognize its realization in an other, its manifestation, to cognize the Logos and the idea. From here follows the necessary transition to philosophy, and specifically to absolute logic.

We defined the absolute first principle as that which possesses the positive force of being. In this definition *implicite* is asserted, first, that the absolute first principle in and of itself is free from every kind of being, and second, that it contains in itself every type of being in a certain aspect, specifically in its positive force or creating principle. These are, as indicated, only two inseparable sides of one and the same definition, since freedom from every kind of being (positive nothingness) presupposes possession of every kind of being. The absolute is free from all kinds of definitions because it, in containing all of them in itself, is inexhaustible and is not eclipsed by them, but rather remains itself. If it were not to possess being, to be deprived of it, it could not as well be free from it — on the contrary, being would then be for it a necessity (since in that case being would not depend on it, but that which does not depend on me, which is given apart from me, is for me a necessity, which I must endure whether I desire it or not).

Thus the absolute is nothing and everything: nothing, in that it is not something, and everything, in that it cannot be devoid of anything. This amounts to one and the same thing, since everything, in not being something, is nothing, and on the other hand, nothing that is (a positive nothing) can be only everything.[b] If it is nothing, then being for it is something else, and if along with this it is the principle of being (as possessing its positive force), then it is the principle of its other. If the absolute were to remain only itself, excluding its other, then this other would be its negation, and as a consequence it itself would no longer be absolute. In other words, if it were to assert itself only as the absolute, then precisely for this reason it could not be the absolute, since in that case its other, the not-absolute,

---

b. This positive nothing, or En-Sof of the Kabbalists, is a direct opposite of the Hegelian negative nothing = pure being, which occurs through the simple abstraction or deprivation of all positive attributes.

would be outside of it as its negation or boundary, and as a consequence it would be limited, exclusive, and not free. In this manner, in order to be what it is, it must be in opposition to its own self or the unity of itself and its opposite —

denn Alles muss in Nichts zerfallen,
Wenn es im Seyn beharren will.[3]

This supreme logical law is only an abstract expression for the great physical and moral fact of love. Love is the self-denial of a being, the affirmation by it of an other, and meanwhile by means of this self-denial its highest self-affirmation is realized. The absence of self-denial or love, i.e., egotism, is not a real self-affirmation of a being, it is only a fruitless, unsatisfiable striving or effort toward self-assertion, as a consequence of which egotism is indeed the source of all kinds of suffering; genuine self-affirmation is attained only in self-denial, and hence both of these definitions are necessarily opposite to their own selves. Thus, when we say that the absolute first principle by its very definition constitutes a unity of itself and its negation, we are repeating, only in a more abstract form, the words of the great apostle: God is love.

As striving toward another absolute, i.e., toward being, love is the principle of plurality, since the absolute in and of itself, as the superexistent, is unconditionally indivisible; moreover, every kind of being is a relationship, and a relationship presupposes those which relate to it, i.e., plurality. But the absolute, being the principle of its other or the unity of itself and this other, i.e., love, cannot, as we have seen, stop being its own self; on the contrary, as in our human love, which is the negation of our I, this I not only does not get lost, but it also receives the highest affirmation, so here as well, in assuming its other; the absolute first principle by that very thing is affirmed as such in its own definition.

Thus the absolute necessarily in all of eternity is distinguished in two poles or two centers: the first is the principle of unconditional unity or individuality as such, the principle of freedom from all kinds of form, from every manifestation, and, it follows, from all of being; the second is the principle or generating force of being, i.e., of the multiplicity of forms. On the one hand, the absolute is higher than every kind of being, is the unconditional unity, the positive nothing; on the other hand, it is the spontaneous potential of being or the first matter. This is because if it were only the superexistent, or free from being, then it could not generate being, and being would not exist; but if being did not exist, then the absolute could not be free from it, since it is impossible to be free from nothing, and, it follows, the absolute itself as such would not exist, and there would not be anything at all — but since there exists something, then necessarily the absolute exists as well in its two poles. The second pole is essence or *prima materia* of the absolute, while the first pole is the absolute itself as such, the positive nothing (En-Sof); this is not some new substance separate from the absolute, but it itself, affirmed as such through the affirmation of its opposite. The absolute, not being subjected in and of itself to any definition (since its general concept as a preliminary exists only for us), defines itself, manifesting itself as an unconditional unity by the assuming of its opposite; since the genuine unity is that which does not exclude multiplicity but, to the contrary, produces it in itself, and moreover, is not violated by it, but remains what it is, remains a unity and by this proves that it is *unconditionally a unity,* a unity in its very essence, not capable of being taken away or destroyed by any multiplicity. If the unity were such only through the absence of multiplicity, i.e., the simple deprivation of multiplicity, and consequently, with the introduction of it, would lose its characteristic of unity, then evidently this unity would only be accidental and not unconditional, the multiplicity would have power over the unity, and it [the unity] would be subordinate to it. A genuine, unconditional unity is necessarily stronger than multiplicity, surpasses it and must demonstrate or realize this superiority, creating in itself every kind of multiplicity and constantly triumphing over it, since everything is tested by its opposite. Thus our spirit is unified not in order to be deprived of its multiplicity, but to the contrary, because in manifesting in itself an endless multiplicity of feelings, thoughts, and desires, it nevertheless always remains itself, and communicates the character of its spiritual unity to this entire elemental multiplicity of phenomena, making the multiplicity its own, belonging to the spirit alone.

> Freedom, captivity, rest, and agitation
> Pass by and once again appear,
> But he is still alone, and in elemental striving
> Only his power is revealed.[4]

Thus, if there is a negative nothing that is negative, which is lesser than being, only the absence, the deprivation of being, constitutes a positive nothing, which is greater or higher than being, possesses power over being, is the genuine freedom from it, then in precisely the same way there is a negative unity that is lesser or lower than multiplicity, there is only the absence or deprivation of it, and there is a positive unity, which is greater or higher than multiplicity — because it possesses power over it, cannot be harmed by it, and consequently is absolutely free from it; it is clear that we must characterize the absolute first principle as a *positive* nothing and a *positive* unity.

The first pole of the absolutely-existent, being in and of itself unconditionally solitary, does not require further explanation, but we must stop at the ambiguous and multifaceted character of another center.

We have seen that the absolutely-existent generally is defined as possessing the power and might of being. This power it possesses is indeed a second center, i.e., a spontaneous, closest, or second potential of being, while the absolute itself, or first center, as possessing it or having power over it, is a remote, or primary, potential of being. The second potential belongs to the absolute first principle by its very definition, and is its own essence. Thus it eternally finds in itself its opposite, since only through the relationship to this opposite can it affirm its own self, hence they are completely interrelated. This is consequently necessity, a divine fate. The absolute first principle is free, only eternally triumphing over this necessity, i.e., remaining unified and unchanged in all the multifaceted creative works of its essence or love. Freedom and necessity thus are correlative — the first being real only through the realization of the second. And since divine necessity, in exactly the same way as the realization of it, is eternal, then similarly eternal is divine freedom; i.e., the absolute first principle as such is never subordinated to necessity, eternally triumphs over it, and thus the eternal unity of freedom and necessity, of itself and an other, constitutes the proper character of the absolute.

> Unified, integral, indivisible,
> Full of its own creation,
> Over it and in it imperturbably
> The divine reigns through the ages.
> In it was clearly realized,
> What no one could comprehend:
> The incompatible is compatible,
> The past fused with the future,

Concept of the Absolute

Creative work combined with rest,
And love with calmness.
And there appear in eternal formation
Its creations again and again.
Always distinct from the universe,
Eternally joined with it,
For the heart it is without question,
For the mind it is clear.[5]

When we speak about necessity in the absolute, evidently there is nothing in common with the external, burdensome necessity of our material existence. Since the absolute cannot have anything that is external or alien to itself, it is its own necessity, its essence, as we stated — it is necessity in the sense that it is necessary for us to live, feel, and love. It is evident that this kind of necessity in no wise contradicts absolute perfection and freedom, but to the contrary, is presupposed by them. Just as evident is the groundlessness of many theologians, who without fail want to deprive divinity of this necessity. If they could only be consistent — just ask them if it is necessary for God to be good, wise, be God, in general exist, and they will be forced to answer in the affirmative. But if it is necessary for God to be, for the same reason it is necessary for him to manifest himself, all the more so, since by the general acknowledgment of the theologians themselves, in him potential is the very act, and indeed all the characteristics they attribute to him relate to something else, and without this not only cannot be realized but also do not possess any meaning at all; and if these characteristics (for example, omnipotence, goodness, fairness, etc.) are essential, then something else is essential as well (i.e., creation), to which they relate. In general, all these questions — Does God create arbitrarily? Could he choose not to create? Could he bring into being not the creation that actually exists but some other kind? and the like — presuppose an extremely childish notion of divinity and give rise only to empty talk completely unworthy of serious minds. But let us leave the speculating theologians to their own sad fate and return to our subject.

The second center or spontaneous potential of being is that which in ancient philosophy was called the "first matter." The matter of every kind of being in reality is not yet being, but neither is it any longer nonbeing — it is specifically the potential of being. Both centers — the absolute as such and the *materia prima*[6] — are different from being, are not themselves being, are both likewise not nonbeing, and since a third state between nonbeing and being is conceivable only as the potential of being, both centers in the same way are defined as the potential of being. But the first is a positive potential, the freedom of being — the superexistent — while the second or material center, being the necessary gravitation toward being, is its negative spontaneous potential, i.e., the affirmed or tangible absence or lack of actual being. But the lack of being as real or tangible (since we are dealing not with abstract or empty words) is the inclination or striving toward being, the craving for being.

In speaking about the first matter as inclination or striving, i.e., in designating it as something internal, psychic, I obviously do not have in mind what contemporary scientists call "matter." I am adhering to the usage of the word accepted in philosophy, and not in chemistry and mechanics, which are not concerned with the first principles or generating forces of being that constitute the subject solely of philosophy. It is obvious that the matter of physics or chemistry, possessing diverse qualities and quantitative relationships, representing, consequently, already some kind of definite and organized being, has a subjective and phenomenal character; consequently, it is in no wise properly matter of the pure potential of being, and in general cannot belong to first principles or the organized elements of that which is existent. The genuine matter about which I am speaking is that ὕλη of ancient philosophers, which in and of itself does not represent and in its conception cannot represent either definite quality or definite quantity; and it is entirely clear that such matter possesses a character that is internal, psychic, or subjective, since that which does not have a definite quality cannot also exert definite action on an other, i.e., of objective being; consequently, it is bounded by subjective being. The psychic character of matter in and of itself begins, incidentally, to be acknowledged even by contemporary scientists, the more thoughtful among whom reduce matter to dynamic atoms, i.e., to the centers of the forces; the idea of force belongs entirely to the subjective or psychic field. What, then, in reality is force in and of itself, i.e., from within, if not a striving or inclination? Such a conception of matter is completely, by the way, compatible with the ordinary, unscientific use of the word. We say in actuality: material inclinations or instinct, material interests, wishes, even material intellect, having in mind, moreover, to be sure, not the matter of physicists or chemists, but precisely the lower side or pole of a psychic entity.

From the aforementioned it is clear that if the highest or free center is the self-affirmation of the absolute first principle as such, then for this self-affirmation it is logically necessary for it to have in itself or as a part of itself its other, its second pole, i.e., the first matter, which for this reason, on the one hand, must be understood as belonging to the first principle, controlled by it, and consequently subordinated to it, while on the other hand, it must be understood as a necessary condition of its existence — matter is more preeminent than it, the absolute first principle depends on matter. On the one hand, the first matter is only the necessary belonging of the free existent, and without it cannot be conceived; on the other hand, it is the free existent's first substratum, its foundation (basis), without which it could not manifest itself or be as such. Thus these two centers, although eternally different and opposite relative to each other, cannot be conceived separately from each other or in and of themselves. They are eternally and inseparably linked with each other, presuppose each other as interrelated, and each is both the begetter and the begotten of the other.

The second pole of the absolute may be defined as *materia prima*, only examined in and of itself or in its potential separateness. In its actual existence — as defined by the existent or as the bearer of its manifestation, as its eternal image — this is the idea. The absolute cannot actually exist other than as realized in its other. This other likewise cannot actually exist in and of itself separately from the absolute first principle, since in this separateness it is pure nothing (since in the absolute there is everything), and pure nothing cannot exist. Thus, if we distinguish another principle in and of itself from this same other as what is determined by the existent, distinguish the first matter from the idea, this constitutes a distinction in reflection but not separateness in existence. That which is the genuinely absolutely-existent eternally resides in its matter or idea as in its realization, manifestation, and embodiment, being eternally distinguished from it and inseparably united with it, and consequently likewise this idea exists eternally in all its fullness as an actual realization, manifestation, or adequate image of the existent. Consequently, the internal relationship of these two centers as well, i.e., the particular ideas or ideal essences that are examined in our logic, have the character of eternal, necessary, and universal truths; here there cannot be any process, any temporal continuity, and if we cannot at once in a single image imagine the entire fullness of the absolute manifested in the idea, the entire reality of their eternal interrelationship, but must account for this interrelationship in its component parts, consistently breaking it down into its separate characteristics, starting from the most general and those with the greatest potential and concluding with the most concrete and actual, then this, as has already been noted, depends solely on the discursive character of our dialectical thinking that is carried out in time, and in no wise determines the particular reality of the absolute itself and its eternal idea. All the diverse characteristics revealed by our dialectics in the idea of the existent actually exist in it, but not separately in rank and file, as we conceive of them, but all at once, in a single eternal living image, the way in which we may only mentally contemplate it.

In distinguishing being from the existent as the principle that generates being and is in possession of it, while in the existent itself distinguishing two centers or poles (the existent as such and the first matter), we thus have three characteristics: (1) the free existent (the superexistent as such), the positive might of being (the first center); (2) necessity of the spontaneous force of being (the first matter, second center); and (3) being or reality as their mutual creation or interrelationship. The second characteristic, in distinction from the third, I call *essence*. Insofar as essence is defined by the existent, essence is its *idea;* insofar as being is defined by the existent, being is its *nature*. If in general everything else deriving from the existent as such or God may be called "being," then we must in any case distinguish proper being or reality from essence or necessity; nature from idea; and natural being from ideal being.

Thus we have: *the existent, essence, being;* or *might, necessity, reality;* or *God, idea,* and *nature*. It is evident that being or nature and essence or idea have between themselves what is common with respect to the existent or God, that both of them are its or his other, and if, as we have just stated, in general everything else deriving from the existent may be called "being," then essence is only an aspect of being, and in that case we will have initially the simple opposition of two categories, the existent and being, and subsequently already in being we will distinguish (1) its means or *modus* (subordinate being, nature) and (2) its content (objective being, idea, essence).

If, as we saw in the previous chapter, even the distinction between being and essence is in general poorly understood in academic philosophy, then in that philosophical tradition the distinction between the two fundamental forms of being, or according to my use of the words, between being and essence, is understood to an even lesser extent. Meanwhile, this distinction is perfectly clear even for an untrained mind. If, for example, when I think, my thinking as a characteristic of my personal being or a certain *modus* of my subjective nature is a certain being, and if likewise the content or subject of my particular thinking, that about which I am thinking, or objective cause, formally determining my thinking, is likewise called "being," then it is evident that here this word is used in two different meanings. My thought and all other subjective being represent the necessary relationship to something; it is impossible just to think, just to want, etc.; that to which I am referring, the objective content of my being, in and of itself can no longer be a relationship. For this reason, it is better to designate this objective content as a distinct category of essence, reserving the category of being for the first form. The circumstance that in each given instance in our apparent reality it is impossible to set an unconditional boundary between these two designations — since here they are intermingled and irrepressibly flow into each other — in no wise should trouble us. This is because logic is concerned with the true character of conceivable definitions as pure expressions of the absolute Logos, and not with their material existence in complex and diversely conditioned phenomena of this world, which in logic can provide only examples but not foundations. From the fact that in this glass of water we cannot mechanically separate and delimit hydrogen from oxygen, does it follow that these elements are inherently indistinguishable? A known substance has in the chemistry laboratory a completely different significance from what is associated with it in the kitchen. Logic is likewise a science — it is the chemistry of the conceived world — and its attributes in no wise depend on the alogical material of our illusory reality.

The relationship we described of the existent to essence and being presupposes an original distinction in the existent itself, i.e., in the first center. This first center, as we have seen, is the self-affirmation of the absolutely-existent, or God, as such on the basis of essence and through being, its self-location, or self-manifestation. Every kind of self-manifestation contains from the perspective of that which is being manifested, three necessary, general aspects: (1) that which is being manifested in itself or of itself, in which the manifestation consists of a concealed, or potential, state; (2) the manifestation as such, i.e., the affirmation of itself in an other or on an other, the discovery, definition, or expression of what is manifested, its Word, or Logos; and (3) the return of that which is being manifested into itself, or the self-discovery of that which is being manifested in manifestation. The absolute self-in-itself existent (1) necessarily differentiates itself, (2) in this differentiation remains itself, and (3) affirms itself as such. It is evident that the absolutely-existent or first center may manifest itself, and consequently differentiate itself in these three forms only with respect to its other or second center, which generates matter or the substance of manifestation. Thus we have three positive principles in the absolutely-existent as the first center, three essential forms or aspects of its manifestation, and also a fourth, negative principle or its other, our second center; being or nature does not belong to the number of first principles in its relative and derivative meaning.

To avoid inconsistency, we must designate by their own names each of the positive principles of the supreme Trinity. For the first center we will retain the term "En-Sof" (positive nothing); the proper character of the second principle cannot be better conveyed than by the term "Word" or "Logos";[c] and the third principle we will call the "Holy Spirit."

Among these first principles of the existent, the one that properly generates it, gives it content, is Logos as the principle of definition, differentiation, inner development, and revelation — the principle of light, in which the entire content of the absolute is revealed or becomes visible (φαίνεται);[7] the two other positive ones, and likewise the fourth negative principle, are accessible and cognizable only insofar as they are defined by Logos, and consequently only through it, in and of themselves, are they hidden and unattainable in their subjective depths. The absolute in and of itself in the first and second principles is unattainable as a hyperbolic negation of itself or an other (the fourth principle or second center — the first matter), and elusive in and of itself as alogical (or hypological).

The fundamental characteristics or distinctions themselves of the existent, essence, and being are possible only through Logos: in the absolute in and of itself, i.e., in En-Sof and the Holy Spirit,[d] they do not exist. If in reality being necessarily is the relationship to something else, while essence

---

c. Since the first principle contains potentially the second, and eternally leads and gives birth to it out of itself as its eternal manifestation, it can be called its "eternal Father," with respect to whom the second principle, or Logos, is the eternal Son.

d. En-Sof is the absolute in and of itself before the manifestation; the Holy Spirit is the absolute in its own self upon the manifestation (it goes without saying, before and upon/during its essence, and not in time); Logos is the absolute not in and of itself, but in manifestation. For this reason, when I say "the absolute in and of itself," I have in mind only the first and third principles. Hence it is easy to see that only Logos has a direct relationship to the fourth principle or first matter, and defines it as idea, about which we will say more at the proper time.

Concept of the Absolute

is none other than this something else, then the absolute as such, not having anything outside itself, is higher than being, and essence consists of its own being — its being is not distinguishable from it as the existent.

Thus Logos, or Word, is the sole objective, i.e., existing for an other, principle of being and knowledge.

In the beginning was the Word, and the Word was with God, and God was the Word. Everything was born through him, and without him nothing was born. That which was born in him was life, and life was the light of the people, and light in the darkness was illuminated, and the darkness did not envelop it.

The Logos realizes the absolute, too, as such, and also the first matter. By means of it, or through it, the absolute is defined as the existent, the first matter — as essence, and the relationship between them — as being, or more precisely, as the means or form of being.

The existent, essence or content, and being or *modus* of existence[e] are the three first logical categories, common to everything that exists. When I affirm something as existing, for example, when I say, "*I am*," in this expression is implied: (1) I as an existing being or the subject of being; (2) a certain means *(modus)* or form of being; since I cannot merely be or be *in general*, I must have a certain specific being, I must be this way or that way, I must possess these or those characteristics, I must have one or another nature; in the present case I am a thinking, desiring, etc., entity, i.e., my being (mode of being) or nature is thought, will, etc., and consequently *I am* means here *I think, desire*, etc. But, (3) I cannot merely think, merely desire or think, or desire in general: I must think about *something*, desire something; i.e., my thinking and desiring are characterized not only as such, subjectively, or as the mode of my subjective being, but also objectively in

---

e. By "being" one can understand not the mode but the very act of existence, but this last as something completely spontaneous does not lend itself to any logical definition. Here the last coincides with the first, and I need only recall the aforementioned at the beginning of this chapter regarding the proper activity of the absolute. In his *Phänomenologie des Geistes*,[8] Hegel superlatively proves the impossibility of logically defining the unmediated reality or sensual authenticity, *Sinnliche Gewissheit* (see *Phänomenologie des Geistes*, 2nd ed., 71-82).[9] But when on this basis Hegel directly negates unmediated reality, it is easy to see that this negation derives only from his exclusive point of view, for which the logical element is everything and the alogical does not exist at all. For every other point of view the alogical character of unmediated reality in no wise interferes with its existence, and between the two extremes the Hegelian "Gefühl ist Alles" is in the final analysis better than the Hegelian "Gefühl ist Nichts."[10]

their content or ideal essence. What I think and what I desire are the objective content or essence of my being and constitute a particular, necessary, and independent moment of my existence, not reduced to what has come before but, to the contrary, defining it.

Thus, the existent, essence, being. This last is properly the manifestation or revelation of the first two by means of the Logos,[f] and for this reason from it (i.e., being), it is more convenient to undertake the development of successive logical categories. Being is the relationship between the existent as such and essence or the first matter. This matter is not the existent as such, but rather the existent's other; but it belongs to the other as its force — the existent is the positive principle of matter as well; it is consequently the principle of its other. The principle of its other is will. That which I posit to be my will is my own, but along with this it constitutes an other, different from myself; otherwise, I could not posit it. Thus, the first relationship of the existent to essence or the first definition of being we have as will.

However, in supposing as its will essence as its own and an other, the existent distinguishes it not only from itself as such but also from its own will. For the existing being to be able to desire this other, it must be in a certain way already given to the being or possessed by it; the other must already exist for the existing being, i.e., be imagined by it or appear to it. Thus essence defines[g] the being of the existent not only as will but also as representation. This representation is its self-representation, since the represented essence as well is its own essence, and in that sense its representation may be called "self-consciousness." However, self-consciousness is defined as such only in distinction from the consciousness of other, external things, and since in the absolute this distinction cannot exist, it is better to retain the term "representation" as the more general one.

Essence cannot be the subject of the will of the existent, not being imagined by it. To be sure, the character and content of this representation are defined by the distinctive Logos of the absolute — this is its own activity. Essence as the other or first matter is only the principle, stimulating this activity and being subordinate to it (*substratum*, ὑποκείμενον). It is not the existent that receives from the representation its content from es-

---

f. In this sense being is the self-definition of Logos, while the existent is that which is defined by Logos as "En-Sof," and essence is that which is defined by Logos as "first matter."

g. More precisely, Logos through essence defines, etc.

sence, but to the contrary, this last, being defined by absolute Logos, receives from it its entire content and becomes actually essence, being inherently only empty matter or the pure potential of being. Therefore, if we call this potential "essence" and "content," then it is not in and of itself, not taken in the abstract, but as already defined by Logos in the potential's relationship to the existent.

The representation of the absolute as defining its essence is thus active, analogous to what we possess in ourselves as imagination.

It is evident that, regarding representation as the state or action of the absolutely-existent itself, there is no significance in the distinctions existing in our representations or what the distinctions are between real (objective) representation and the fantastic, or illusory; and furthermore between a contemplative (perceptible) representation and an abstract representation, or properly speaking, thinking (in general terms); the significance is between objective or cognitive thinking and subjective thinking, or opinion. These distinctions derive from the fact that every finite entity, being only a detached part of the whole, possesses outside of itself an entire world of already defined essences, an entire world of being independent of the given entity. This world in its action determines the representations of each separate entity, which (the representations) only with respect to this determining cause possess objective meaning; aside from this cause they are only states of subjective consciousness.

What we apprehend as the action of external essences through external being, i.e., through a complex interrelationship of diverse essences independent of us, we call "external experience" and thus distinguish the objective world independent of us from the subjective world of our internal states. This distinction, as we will see subsequently, is completely relative and subject to dialectic transformation, but nevertheless for us it exists. For the absolute, as not possessing outside of itself any actual definite being, all of reality is reduced to its own states and actions, and here the distinction of the subjective from the objective, transferred wholly into the internal sphere, is determined by its own will. Insofar as the represented essence not only is represented but also is affirmed by the will of the existent, to that same extent does the essence acquire the meaning of its own reality and as such exert an influence on the existent.

The exertion of influence on the existent by means of its already determined representation and by the will of essence gives a new definition to its being as feeling.

PRINCIPLES OF ORGANIC LOGIC (CONTINUATION)

For finite entities there are two kinds of interactions of objective being (representations) with the subjective (will): first, the interaction of external empirical reality or objective material representations with our material physical subject, i.e., with our animal organism, which is nothing other than the manifestation of unconscious material desire; this first interaction produces sensations of external feelings, and an external or corporal sensuality; and second, the interaction of our internal objectivity, i.e., of our thoughts,[h] with our internal subjective being, i.e., with our personal conscious will — this causes so-called internal feeling. It is understandable that in the absolutely-existent this distinction cannot exist, and that consequently in it internal and external feeling, spiritual and corporal sensuality, coincide.

Thus we have three basic categories, by which are defined the direct relationship of the existent to its other or essence, or three basic attributes of its being. It desires its own essence, imagines it, feels it; hence its being is characterized as *will, imagination, feeling*. What constitutes properly will, imagination, and feeling — this is known to us from our immediate consciousness, and for this reason cannot be in question. But how then must we understand that other, to which the existent in its being relates as to its essence?

As we have seen, the other inherently does not possess any reality; separate from the existent, it is pure possibility or the potential of being, matter, ὕλη, μὴ ὄν.[11] This means that it really does not exist at all outside the existent or separately from it, but rather is located in it as its own potential negation similar to the way we in ourselves find our material nature as the internal negation of our own spiritual I (it goes without saying that this is only an analogy, and not an exact sameness of relationships). This potential may be realized only by an internal act of the very existent itself, by its will. This is possible and necessary for the existent, for the very reason that it by its definition possesses the positive force of being, and being is possible only in relationship to essence as its realization. This realization gives to material potential a certain relative independence, makes it similarly an actual force, but a passive force, capable of being defined by the existent and of influencing it. Therefore, the primary distinction of the absolute

---

h. If our thinking with respect to external reality is something subjective, then with respect to our will it represents an objective element. It is evident that these attributes are completely relative.

into two centers or two polar forces becomes real, and all of reality possesses, it is evident, its own positive principle only in the first center, while in the second it is perceived and passively formed. Without this distinction the existent would not possess the basis for its manifestation and would have to, so to speak, act in emptiness, which is inconceivable; thus the *materia prima* in the aforementioned meaning is necessary, as being determined by the existent through the absolute Logos as its object; this *materia prima* is called "idea."

It is evident that idea as such must be distinguished according to the distinctions in the being of the existent, which (being) is only the relationship of the existent to it (idea). Idea is namely that which the existent desires, what it imagines, what it feels or senses — this is its own subject or content. As the content of the will of the existent, the idea is *the good;* as the content of its imagination it is *truth;* as the content of its feeling it is *beauty.* For the time being we accept these definitions as general concepts or conditional signs for a certain real, concrete content that we will utilize in further development. By means of this, our philosophy distinguishes itself in the given relationship from that academic idle talk that accepts the ideas of the good, truth, and beauty in their abstraction as certain valid and, moreover, inherently existing principles that compose a *summa philosophiae.* Schopenhauer legitimately ridiculed such idle talk. Even more deserving of mockery are those theologians who intend with this abstract trilogy to cover the Christian doctrine of the Trinity and, in having called the Father "the good," the Son "truth," and the Holy Spirit "beauty," imagine that by these words everything has been said.

The existent in its unity already contains in itself potential will, imagination, and feeling. But for these modes of being actually to be realized as such, it is necessary for them to differentiate themselves, and for this it is essential for the existent to affirm them in their particularity or, more precisely, to affirm itself in them as particular, as a consequence of which they would appear as independent relative to each other. But since these modes of being by their very nature are inextricably connected with each other, because it is impossible to desire without imagining or feeling, impossible to imagine without will or feeling, etc., the existent cannot affirm these modes of being in their simple separateness in such a way that first, *only* will would be affirmed, second, *only* imagination, and third, *only* feeling. It follows, then, that they cannot be isolated in and of themselves, while the distinctive feature necessary for their actual realization may consist only in

PRINCIPLES OF ORGANIC LOGIC (CONTINUATION)

the differentiation of the existent itself, as first, *predominantly willing,* second, *predominantly imagining,* and third, *predominantly feeling;* i.e., in affirming itself in its will, the existent along with will possesses imagination and feeling, but as aspects subordinated to the will; second, in affirming itself in imagination, the existent possesses along with it will and feeling, but again as aspects already subordinated to imagination; finally, in affirming itself in feeling, the existent possesses along with it will and imagination, but as aspects already defined by and subordinated to feeling. In other words, imagination, being isolated from will, necessarily receives its own will and feeling (since this last is isolated by the influence of what is imagined on the will), and consequently, what is imagining as such becomes a particular and integral subject. Furthermore, feeling, being isolated from will and imagination, as a consequence of which, emerges as an independent and complete subject. Finally, will, in having separated out from itself imagination and feeling as such, by this same necessarily receives its own particular imagination and feeling, and what is willing as such emerges as a particular and integral subject.

Thus the Logos of the absolute, by the law of its manifestation separating out the diverse forms or modes of being, separates the existent as well into three subjects, each of which is defined especially by one of the fundamental modes of being, but not exclusively; rather, it is defined jointly with the two others only as secondary or subordinate elements. The logical necessity of such isolation in the existent, indicated above in brief, I hope, will become apparent after the following explanation.

As soon as the three basic modes of being are given, their relationship to the existent as to a subject for which they are predicates may be threefold. First, they may be[i] predicates only of one subject. In that case this single subject will possess will, imagination, and feeling in equal measure. And what constitutes the content of this will, imagination, and feeling? It goes without saying, its own primary essence in three basic forms or ideas — the good, truth, and beauty. But as we know, this primary essence in and of itself is only *materia prima* or pure potential and cannot by itself give itself any attributes, but only receive or apprehend them, so the three basic ideas in their positive content are defined in general by the action of the existent, specifically, as we will soon see, by the real interrelationships of the various subjects of being or the various existents. But since in our

---

i. Here I have in mind possibility in its most general, abstract meaning.

present supposition these various subjects, or existents, are specifically not allowed, but only a single one, then ideas in their positive content may in the face of this be defined solely by this one subject; i.e., the good as such is defined exclusively by the subject's will, truth as such exclusively by the subject's imagination, and beauty as such exclusively by the subject's feeling; in other words, in the face of this supposition the good is the good only because the subject desires it, truth is truth only because the subject imagines it, and beauty is beauty only because the subject feels it; consequently, in response to the question about the content or object of the subject's will, imagination, and feeling, we could answer here only that the subject wants what it wants, imagines what it imagines, and feels what it feels, or that it *simply* wants, *simply* imagines, *simply* feels. But this does not make any sense, and consequently our supposition as leading to such an absurd conclusion must be acknowledged as false.

According to the second possible supposition, each of the three modes of being possesses a particular subject that, moreover, corresponds to it exclusively. The willing subject possesses only the predicate of will, and of nothing else; the imagining subject possesses only the predicate of imagination, and nothing more; and the feeling subject possesses exclusively the predicate of feeling. But, on the one hand, such exclusivity would contradict the nature of these predicates themselves, because, as was already noted, wanting as such necessarily presupposes imagination and feeling, and likewise with imagination and feeling, each in its turn presupposes the two other modes of being. On the other hand, such exclusivity is impossible with respect to supposed subjects as well. If in actuality a given subject were only the willing (while the second were only the imagining and the third were only the feeling), then the predicate of will (of imagination, of feeling), in being the absolute definition of a subject, occupying it wholly, would exclude its freedom, so it could no longer be a real independent subject;[j] meanwhile, the subject's reality as such is necessary also for the reality of the predicate itself.

Thus, the second supposition as well turns out to be inconceivable, leaving only the third, i.e., if three subjects are necessary and if these three subjects cannot be differentiated among themselves by the three predicates

---

j. At the same time that in the context of the multiplicity of predicates the being of one of them frees the subject from the exclusive power of another, and by means of this asserts its independence.

belonging exclusively to each of them, since by the nature of these predicates themselves, and equally by the nature of the subject in general, such exclusivity is impossible, then each subject must possess all the predicates, differentiating itself from the others only by the differing interrelationship of these predicates.

Concerning the very differentiation of the three integral subjects, for a sensory imagination it may be represented in the form of the integration of parts. I have in mind that if we imagine three basic aspects of being as elements or component parts in the being of the existent, then as soon as, according to the law of Logos, each of these parts separates from the others or affirms itself in its uniqueness, the existent necessarily completes each one by the creation of the two others, and integrating them, thus itself breaks up into three particular and concrete subjects. We encounter individual examples of this kind of integration as well in nature, in our material world. Thus, everyone knows *si licet magnis comparare parva*,[12] that if one cuts the body of a sea hydra or an earthworm into pieces, each piece will quickly become integrated, completing itself with all the missing organs, and as a result several whole organisms, instead of one, will emerge.

Thus we have three independent and integral subjects of being, or three existents, to each of which belong all three basic modes of being, but only in a different relationship. In the first subject imagination and feeling are subordinated to will; in other words, it imagines and feels, only insofar as it wants to, which already necessarily follows from its original meaning. In the second, which already has the first as a precedent, what predominates is the objective element of imagination, the defining cause of which is the first subject; will and feeling are subordinated here to imagination: it desires and feels, only insofar as it imagines. In the third subject, which already has as a precedent both the magical being of the first subject and the ideal being of the second, a particular or independent significance can belong only to real or sensual being: it imagines and wants, only insofar as it feels.

The first subject or first specificity of the existent as such I call "spirit" (πνεῦμα, *spiritus*); the second, "mind" (Νοῦς, *intellectus* or *mens*); the third, "soul" (ψυχή, *anima*).

Thus, *spirit, mind, soul.*

The spirit is the existent as the subject of will and the bearer of the good, and as a consequence of this or because of it likewise is the subject of the imagination of truth and the feeling for beauty. The mind is the existent as the subject of imagination and the bearer of truth, and as a consequence of this likewise is the subject of the will, the good, and the feeling for beauty. The soul is the existent as the subject of feeling and the bearer of beauty, and as a consequence of this is only or to a certain extent subordinated similarly to the will of the good and the imagination of truth.

I will explain this relationship with an example from human experience. There are people who, having fallen in love with someone right away, already on the basis of this love conceptualize a general impression of the beloved object, and likewise because of the strength and degree of this love determine as well the aesthetic value of the impressions given rise to by the beloved entity. But there are also people in whom each given entity brings forth at first a certain general theoretical impression of themselves, and already this impression conforms to their will and feeling concerning this entity. Finally, there are also people on whom first and foremost the sensual aspect of an object acts, and by means of aesthetic effects both their intellectual and moral relationships to the object are already determined. The first group at first loves or desires, and consequently already because of its love or will imagines and feels; the second group at first imagines, and by means of this imagination already desires and feels; the third group first and foremost feels, and according to feeling already imagines and desires. The first are spiritual people, the second intellectual people, the third psychic or sensual people.*

We have three independent subjects or hypostases — *single-principled people,* since for them everything derives from one absolute first principle; *people of a single essence,* insofar as they all possess one common essence or primary matter concerning which only they can be independent, receiving from it [the common essence or primary matter] their negative attributes; and *people of a single character* or *people of a single manner* (single-natured), insofar as the same general means or forms of being, the same nature, belong to all of them. The unity of the absolute first principle in no wise is violated by this threefold-ness of subjects, since, as we have seen, the absolute first principle, manifesting itself by means of its Logos, remains in possession of the positive force of being, does not turn into its own manifestation. It is also clear that despite all their independence or particularity, the three primary subjects cannot be equivalent: insofar as

---

*This distinction, indicated here in passing, will take on a rather important significance in ethics.

will in its essence precedes imagination and feeling, and insofar as the good in its essence precedes truth and beauty, to that extent spirit necessarily precedes mind and soul.

Having laid out the threefold-ness of the subjects, we arrive at a certain, albeit still a very general, but already completely definite, meaning of the three basic concepts — the good, truth, and beauty.

The content of the three subjects is the idea. But the idea in and of itself, as the *prima materia,* is something completely indefinite and passive, and in this sense cannot provide objective content; it receives its specificity from the absolutely existent, of which it is an essential reflection. And since the existent itself is manifested in three subjects, the idea may provide positive content for one of these subjects not in and of itself, but only insofar as it is defined by the other subjects or in relationship to them (from which again is seen the necessity of multiple subjects). A subject, it is clear, cannot spontaneously in and of itself or as such become the content of another subject, and consequently the content or idea really consists of their defining of each other; moreover, it is evident that it consists of their *positive* mutual definition, i.e., of their certain *unity.*

Thus, in general *the idea is the objective unity of three subjects,* the substratum of which is essence or primary matter.

As a consequence of the threefold-ness of the fundamental modes of being, the unity or idea as well must be threefold, and it is self-evident that the unity is impossible without free subordination.

The primary good, or idea as the good (the idea of good), is *the unity of will among the first-spirit, first-mind, and first-soul* — in other words, a free subordination of mind and soul to the spirit relative to will, or the potential of their own will, supplying actual being to the will of the spirit. Mind and soul as particular subjects possess their own essential will, which separates them from spirit, but precisely as a consequence of this independence they may freely subordinate themselves to it.

Primary truth, or idea as truth (the idea of truth), *is the unity of imagination among spirit, soul, and mind,* or the free subordination of the first two to the last one relative to imagination. Spirit and soul as a consequence of freedom compose their theoretical force of imagination in a condition of potentiality ceding actual imagination to the mind; i.e., both spirit and soul actually represent only what is assumed by the mind.

Finally, *primary beauty,* idea as beauty or the idea of beauty, *is the unity of feeling among spirit, mind, and soul,* or the free subordination of the first two to the last one relative to feeling. Spirit and mind freely leave their aesthetic force in a state of potential, giving actual feeling to soul; i.e., spirit and mind actually feel only that which takes place in the soul.

Thus the first good is the moral harmony of the three first subjects, or their convergence in a single will; the first truth is their mental harmony, or their convergence in a single imagination; and the first beauty is the sensual or aesthetic harmony of these subjects — their convergence in a single feeling.

Each of these primary subjects as such possesses the force of exclusive self-affirmation, but precisely as a consequence of this it may freely reject this self-affirmation, i.e., it possesses the force of self-negation. Spirit may objectively represent everything it wants, but it freely rejects this arbitrariness and represents only what is assumed by the mind. Similar to this, the primary mind may want everything it imagines, but in reality it wants or affirms from what is imagined by it only what corresponds to the will of absolute spirit. Precisely the same thing may be said about the soul.

Thus the existent spirit is defined by the mind and soul, becomes a potential relative to them, and insofar as it is potential, to that extent its other, i.e., essence or idea, becomes actual, receives a real image. Likewise, mind is defined by spirit and soul, and soul by spirit and mind.

It is in this sense that what the mind and soul receive in the idea from spirit is the good, what the spirit and soul receive in the idea from mind is truth, and what the mind and spirit receive in the idea from soul is beauty.

The spirit desires a complete harmonious essence or idea, and with this desire defines it as the desired, i.e., as the good. Mind and soul likewise want the idea, but do not define it as the desired; rather, they receive it in this capacity from spirit: for them it already exists as the good. But the mind not only wants a complete essence or idea — first and foremost, the mind imagines it and by this same defines it as the imagined, i.e., as truth. Spirit and soul likewise conceive the idea but do not define it as truth: in this capacity for them it is already a given of the mind. The soul feels a complete essence or idea and by means of this defines it as aesthetic, or beauty; the spirit and mind likewise feel idea but do not define it themselves as beauty: in this capacity it is already apprehended by them as the soul.

It is evident that the substratum of these three unities or ideas, to which the three subjects relate harmoniously, is the second center of the absolute, or the primary matter, which in this eternal development is defined as idea in its various forms.

PRINCIPLES OF ORGANIC LOGIC (CONTINUATION)

In and of itself the idea as the other of the existent emerges as pure potential without any objective being, and here may be called "idea" only κατὰ πρόληψιν;[13] its actual definition in this respect is the *materia prima*. The existent emerges here as a pure act, free from any relative being, self-contained, and since this freedom and self-contained-ness make up the character of what is usually called "spirit," here already the existent may be defined as "spirit." This is because although with respect to the other the spirit is defined as predominantly willing, this does not express its own reality. To desire something it is necessary to possess something already, and to desire everything it is necessary in a certain way to possess everything. Simple desire, which does not presuppose any reality in the desiring, does not constitute even will; this materially blind striving is the thirst for being. The absolutely-existent as such possesses everything in a spontaneous act, and therefore its other may be only pure potential in it. Possessing everything in itself, the existent cannot want to create something essentially different — it can desire only to possess its own content as an other. This characterizes every kind of creative work. An artist wants to create not something alien to himself, completely different from himself, what might not exist in him at all — to the contrary, he wants only that idea that is found in himself, that defines his inner being or comprises his own inner content — he wants to realize this idea of his outside of himself, make it an other to himself, differentiate and isolate it. And as the artist, in objectivizing his content or making it external, does not lose it as an internal part of himself, so the absolutely-existent in its manifestation does not cease to remain itself.

Pure, self-contained actuality as a condition that is one-sided and exclusive contradicts the very definition of the absolutely-existent. Therefore it (the absolute) must receive potentiality, provide a place for the other, not losing, it goes without saying, its own reality or its positive force. The absolute may receive potentiality (materiality) or the definition of itself as an other only through its own affirmation of this other, i.e., of the primary matter or nothing, through the communication to it (the other or nothing) of its (absolute) own reality, or positive force, as a consequence of which this nothing or primary matter becomes actual and may act upon the existent as the primary idea.

Insofar as the absolutely-existent is subject to the action of this other or idea realized by it, it is passive, potential, materialized: this materialization is indeed the realized Logos — Λόγος ἔκθετος or προφορικός.[14]

As complete, free from every kind of exclusivity, the existent must communicate to the idea not only a certain reality but also its entire reality, realize it fully, give to it all the form and attributes contained in its positive force. And first and foremost relative to the most general forms or modes of being, the idea emerges not only as desired but also as imagined, not only as imagined but also as felt or real. This is the gradual actualization or formalization (formation) of an idea and, corresponding to it, the gradual potentialization or materialization of the existent, detaching itself into the willing spirit, imagining mind, and feeling soul. In the latter the material element of the existent balances the purely spiritual element, and for this reason the soul may be called *materia secunda*.[15] Corresponding to this, the idea of the soul, i.e., beauty, possesses the highest degree of actuality and the most fullness of formal being; for this reason, it is the last, final manifestation, or realization, of the idea as such. In this sense the good is an affirmed goal, truth is necessarily a defining means, beauty is a real fulfillment, or manifestation; in other words, the existent, in affirming the idea as the good, gives it by means of truth manifestations in beauty.

Every kind of self-defining activity of the existent by means of this produces an other or the idea: it becomes the subject or bearer of the idea. Thus all activity of this kind is the subjectivization of the existent, and along with this or by means of this the objectivization of the primary matter, the transformation of it from pure indefinite potential into specific, definite objective essence or idea. In this sense the idea is last, but on the other hand, only the idea in its potential existence may define the activity of the existent as will, imagination, and feeling. Thus here all principles are inextricably bound up with each other, one necessarily presupposes the other, and all of them together form a single closed circle, which constitutes genuine infinity. Properly speaking, we have four substantial defining principles — spirit, mind, soul, and idea — since the various modes of being, and equally the various forms of the idea, are not principles, but issue only from the interrelationship of the three subjects and the idea, whence it is clear that all of being and all definite essence are necessarily relative. The existent in three subjects is not being, but likewise the idea in and of itself is not being; they receive being only in their interrelationship or interaction, in and of themselves are forces of being; moreover, spirit, mind, and soul are positive and active forces while the idea is a negative and passive force.

Thus the absolute, in its Logos relating to its primary matter, manifests itself according to the categories of the existent, essence, and being in the following basic categories:

I	II	III
the Existent	*Essence*	*Being* (means or *modus*
as such *(God)*	(content or *idea*)	of being, *nature*)
1. Spirit	1. the Good	1. Will
2. Mind	2. Truth	2. Imagination
3. Soul	3. Beauty	3. Feeling

From the aforementioned it is first and foremost clear that all these categories derive their real meaning only in relationship to essence or idea. Idea is thus that in which the absolute realizes itself by means of its Logos; only in it does it with all its categories become substantial, real, and objective. From here it is clear that idea possesses a particular reality not with respect to the absolute in and of itself, for which this reality is only its own self-consciousness or its internal image, but only for Logos, which receives from idea its real force while communicating to it its content. Thus Logos and idea in general are correlative (as the active and passive principle, respectively, as form and matter, etc.), and all the basic attributes of the absolute are expressions of their direct interaction or direct manifestations of Logos in the idea. But it is clear that in these attributes Logos as such expresses itself to varying degrees, and that precisely the special expression of Logos in the idea is truth, with respect to which Logos itself, as the existent, is specifically defined as mind, and the mode of its being as imagination. The remaining attributes are necessarily the expression of Logos, but not as such, not in its particularity. In the attribute of the willing spirit Logos apparently expresses predominantly the quality of the first absolute principle, or En-Sof; in the attribute of feeling soul it expresses predominantly the quality of the third absolute principle, or the Holy Spirit; and only in the attribute of the imagining mind does it manifest its own particularity, its specific character. Corresponding to this in the definition of the good, the idea through Logos takes into itself the reality of the first principle, while in the definition of beauty the idea through Logos is not subject to the action of the third principle, and only in the definition of truth the idea is defined directly by Logos itself as such. If thus the willing spirit and feeling soul are manifestations in the Logos of hyperbolic principles that are inherently free from any difference or multiplicity of forms, then their further definitions or formations may be received by the first essence or idea not from these principles, but only from the representing or imagining mind, and consequently in the idea of truth or as genuine essence, as a result of which the ideas of the good and beauty, remaining inherently unchanged in their internal identity as absolute unities, receive their further development only with respect to the idea of truth or through truth.

Thus we must turn our attention to the articulation of those attributes that the mind gives to idea as genuine essence, which will compose the content of the next chapter.

PART V

Principles of Organic Logic (Continuation): Relative Categories That Define Idea as an Entity

The superexistent absolute, which inherently is positive nothing (En-Sof), is realized or manifested in its other or idea, which thus is the realized or manifested (revealed) superexistent; the very act of manifestation or revelation is Logos, or more precisely, the superexistent in the act of its revelation is Logos.

Every revelation is differentiation; for the absolute, not possessing anything outside of itself, differentiation is self-differentiation. Thus Logos is absolute in its self-differentiation.

Each thing with respect to the absolute first principle of everything that exists may be cognized in a threefold manner: first, in substantial, fundamental, and primary unity with the superexistent, i.e., in pure potentiality or positive nothing (in En-Sof, or God the Father); second, in differentiation from the superexistent or in the act of manifestation (in Logos or the Son); and third, in the free, i.e., mediated, unity with the superexistent (in the Holy Spirit).

When we distinguish categories, we can do this only in Logos; therefore, we do not make such distinctions unconditionally *(condition* is from the word *"logos"*). Every kind of logical cognition is by definition conditional or relative; unconditional logical cognition, unconditional logic, is *contradictio in adjecto*. To cognize logically means to cognize in relation to, i.e., relatively. Logos is a relationship, i.e., originally the relationship of the superexistent to its own self as such or its self-differentiation; since the superexistent is the absolute, i.e., along with it, it is *everything* as well. Logos is likewise the relationship of the superexistent to everything and of everything to the superexistent. The first relationship is the internal or

PRINCIPLES OF ORGANIC LOGIC (CONTINUATION)

concealed Logos (λόγος ἐνδιάθετος); the second is Logos revealed (λόγος προφορικός); the third is Logos embodied or concrete (Christ).

The first Logos cannot be real without the second, nor can the second be real without the third, and all three presuppose that to which the existent relates through them, i.e., its other or essence; moreover, the other or essence corresponds to the first or internal Logos, which in the act is only the self-differentiation of the absolute, only as pure potential or idea in possibility (magic or Maya); the other corresponds to the second or open Logos as pure idea, i.e., in a reality comprehensible to the mind; finally, the concrete idea or Sophia corresponds as well to the third or concrete Logos. The meaning of this third Logos and the ideas corresponding to it may be clarified only later; now we must focus on the first two.

In the absolute the *other* is only the manifested *same;* it only seems (is imagined, seen, appears) an other, and in this respect is *Maya,* i.e., visibility or phantom. But only through this visibility is the real manifestation of the absolute possible; for this reason Maya represents the only possibility or might of creation: Maya = magic. By this same it is the original substratum of everything, or the primary matter.

To this first stage of idea corresponds (as we have seen, from the standpoint of the absolute principle) the internal or concealed Logos, which, being on the one hand, as was stated above, the first stage in the real manifestation of the absolute, or the first of the three Logoi, is along with this the internal principle of self-differentiation in the absolute as such, or the second aspect of the supreme, superessential Trinity. In actuality, the absolutely-existent manifests itself as well in its manifestation; i.e., with respect to its other it is Logos, while as a manifestation, i.e., in the other, it is idea; however, in manifesting itself it necessarily remains its own self or in itself, and in this internal self-affirmation with respect to the manifestation are differentiated three stages — three eternal phases of its own existence. The first is it itself in unconditional undifferentiatedness as the very first logically of every kind of manifestation. We already designated this phase of the absolute existent as "En-Sof," or "God the Father" (protogod); here the existent and its other or essence, and consequently their relationship or being, are not differentiated. The second stage is the absolute as such with respect to the manifestation, i.e., that which differentiates itself as such from its own manifestation; this precisely is the internal or concealed Logos (the open Logos with all its manifestations is rooted in the depths of the absolute, and this — its root — is the internal or first

Relative Categories That Define Idea as an Entity

Logos). Finally, the third phase is the absolute with respect to its own self as already manifested or in relationship with the idea, i.e., the absolutely existent, which, being manifested or embodied, remains itself, remains as the superexistent and by means of this unconditionally affirms itself as such — the Holy Spirit.

Thus, if in general we distinguish the absolute or superexistent itself, then the real or revealed Logos, and finally the idea, then in the absolute itself, in its internal existence, necessarily appears the same kind of threefold differentiation. Moreover, the internal or concealed Logos corresponds here to the external or revealed Logos, while the third, internal phase, i.e., the Holy Spirit, corresponds to the idea.

The basic categories of the existent, essence, and being as general concepts necessarily belong properly to the absolute, and equally so both to Logos and to idea, but to differing degrees and in differing relationships. Properly the absolute is predominantly the existent, then already essence and being; as the existent it is spirit, as being it is will, and as essence the good. Logos is predominantly being, specifically imagination (i.e., the act of imagination), but it likewise is the existent, specifically the mind, and essence, specifically truth. Finally, idea is predominantly essence, specifically beauty, but likewise the existent, specifically the soul, and being, specifically feeling. Although in the previous chapter we sometimes identified the existent with the absolute, essence with idea, and being with Logos, since they really correspond in a certain respect, this is not an absolute identity, which is already impossible here because the existent, essence, and being are general logical categories, necessarily peculiar to everything that exists, albeit to varying degrees, while the properly absolute, Logos, and idea in all their universality possess, as we will see, a completely particular and individual character.

What is of concern here is that among the three principles and basic categories described in the previous chapter there exists a twofold connection: in content and in the form of existence, so that one and the same definition relating in content to Logos or idea, in the form of existence, relates to the absolute, and vice versa. And precisely mind and soul, of which the first in content belongs to Logos while the second belongs to idea, in the form of their existence both, i.e., as existents or forms of the existent, relate to the properly absolute, which is the existent predominantly. Furthermore, will and feeling, of which the first in content belongs to the absolute while the second belongs to idea, in the form of their existence, as aspects of being, relate along with imagination to Logos, which is being predominantly. Finally, the definitions of the good and truth, which in their content belong as follows: the first to the absolute, the second to Logos, while in the form of existence, as essences, they relate together with beauty to idea, which is essence primarily, as a result of which the good and truth are called "ideas" on a level that is equal to that of beauty, although a specifically ideal quality belongs only to beauty.

The twofold connection of the nine (or twelve, if we count the three general categories) basic concepts among themselves and with the three individual principles (the absolute, Logos, and idea) may be expressed in the following table:

(1) the Existent *(Absolute)*	(2) Being *(Logos)*	(3) Essence *(Idea)*
1. the Absolute ... Spirit	Will	the Good
2. Logos .... Mind	Imagination	Truth
3. Idea .... Soul	Feeling	Beauty

Since the absolute or the whole by its definition cannot possess anything outside itself that is essentially foreign to it, its other or idea may be only this same absolute, but only in the form of a different being, i.e., fixed for itself or objectivized, cognized; thus we have: the absolute or manifested for itself (Idea) and the act itself of its manifestation (Logos).

The superexistent principle as such (or the absolute proper) is the unconditionally internal unity, and consequently Idea as the manifested absolute is *the realized unity,* i.e., *unity in everything* or in multiplicity; this everything, this multiplicity, is already contained potentially in the absolute, which is unified and everything. In Logos this potential multiplicity is translated into the act, and therefore in the idea it must again be connected to the unity *as already real.* In other words, the superexistent as such is the fundamental, substantial unity of the many before their manifestation (or more precisely, independently of their manifestation), Idea is their real unity as already manifested, and Logos is the principle of their differentiation.

Concerning these myriad elements themselves, which Logos differentiates in the absolute and which locate their unity within Idea, we have already defined the basic ones among them as spirit, mind, and soul. Thus, Idea is the real unity of spirit, mind, and soul. They are unified in the abso-

Relative Categories That Define Idea as an Entity

lute, and unified as well in Idea, but in a different way. They are substantially unified in the absolute, differentiated in Logos, and unite actually in Idea. Their differentiated being by means of Logos — specifically will as the being of spirit, imagination as the being of mind, and feeling as the being of soul — is called the "nature" or "character" of the existent. Logos is the producing (defining, active) principle of being or nature, and to this extent corresponds to them, but is not identical to them and must not be confused with them. It is divinity in being or nature, the same as Idea is divinity in essence or object (reflection).

The unity of the three basic subjects in Idea emerges as threefold, insofar as the principle of this unity may be found in the properly absolute, or in Logos, or spontaneously in Idea itself. In other words, this unity of theirs, realized in Idea, is different for the absolute than either for Logos or for Idea itself. As we already know, the first is the good, the second is truth, the third is beauty. Only truth, as a theoretical or logical unity, *is thought;* the good as such only *is wanted (desired),* while beauty as such only *is felt.* In other words, the good is the unity of the subjects or Idea, insofar as it is wanted, truth insofar as it is imagined or thought, and beauty insofar as it is felt. Perfect unity is based on the premise that *the identical one,* specifically Idea, that is pondered as truth is also *precisely the same* that is wanted or desired as the good, and likewise the same, not some kind of other, that is felt as beauty; hence these three categories are not some sort of separate entities, but only three forms or aspects, in which for various subjects one and the same thing appears, specifically Idea, in which thus remains the entire fullness of Divinity.

But what actually is this one and the same thing? What constitutes idea, which we desire as the good, which we imagine or ponder as truth, which we perceive as beauty? In other words, what do we desire in the good, what do we ponder in truth, what do we perceive in beauty? It is evident that a logically defined answer is possible only to the second of these three questions, since the good as such and beauty as such, being the objects respectively of will and feeling, and not of thought, do not belong to logical definitions, which relate to idea only as to truth. But as a consequence of the unity of idea we do not need a logical definition of all its forms, since the good and beauty are the same as truth, but only of the modes of will and feeling, and not of the mode of imagination. When we ask: What is beauty? i.e., what content does it possess? we are actually asking: What do we mean by beauty? And since the real subject in question is truth, we are actually asking: What is truth in its relationship to beauty? The same consideration obtains with respect to the question of the good. Thus any theoretical question, i.e., the question of content, regardless of the way it is posed, is always a question about truth and cannot be concerned with anything else.

Since idea in the form of truth is the conceived unity of subjects, the content of this idea depends on the particular characteristics of these subjects or on their conceived differences. If in general the beginning of differentiation is Logos, its unmediated subject is Mind; i.e., Mind directly defined by Logos differentiates itself from other subjects, and these very differences lead to unity in Idea. In this sense Logos defines Idea through Mind. But on the other hand, conditioned by Logos, Mind understands the differences only in light of their unity in Idea; i.e., Idea as a not-yet-defined, potential unity is imagined by Mind in its differentiating activity, and in this sense it is already defined through Idea. Thus this eternal logical process, through which truth is defined, is the interrelationship of Logos and Idea through Mind.

Original Mind conceives Idea in a logical form as truth. Its conception is mental contemplation; i.e., everything that it ponders in Idea possesses a direct objectivity, or more precisely, the opposition between the subjective and the objective does not exist for the original Mind in the sense in which it possesses force for us. For our individual mind as such, i.e., in its self-affirmation, giving birth to purely rational or abstract thought, Idea or essence, i.e., the existent as object, appears only in abstraction as a concept. This is because our mind in its separateness, being only a particular phenomenon among other phenomena and possessing as a consequence first and foremost outside itself an entire objective world not dependent on it, must in its activity — if it truly wants to impart to this activity some sort of objective meaning — subordinate itself to the laws of this objective world that are independent of the mind; it does not have productive force, it cannot *produce* truth, but rather can only *find* it. Idea in the form of truth already has primacy over it [Mind], and moreover it, insofar as it is linked with the empirical being of a concrete person, [this idea] is not given directly in its purity but is intermingled with the secondary, productive, empirical being of things, subordinated to myriad other conditions apart from pure thought; consequently, the first task of our mind consists here of separating idea from empirical admixture, diverting or removing it; but it is evident that to divert or re-

Relative Categories That Define Idea as an Entity

move it is possible only in a form without a subordinate reality, or only as a concept.[a]

Thus there are two kinds of thought or pure imagination: productive or integral, belonging to the original mind (and likewise to ours, insofar as ours becomes a participant in the first), and reflective or abstract thought characteristic of our mind in its self-affirmation.

Idea as truth or in the sphere of the mind, being a conceivable unity or harmony, presupposes conceivable differences, since through the reality of these last evidently the reality of their unity is conditioned as well. The necessity of differences gives us the negative element in the productive activity of the original mind. This is because genuine unity presupposes not simple differentiation or heterogeneity, but opposition or polarity, i.e., their mutual negation. In reality, mere diverse or heterogeneous things and concepts (for example, an isosceles triangle and a musical composition, or the multiplication table and a stearin candle) do not constitute any basis below the possibility of the unmediated interaction and unity, and indifferently remain foreign to each other. On the contrary, homogeneous but opposite or polar terms mutually negated by each other and along with this necessary to the same degree, require a third term that is homogeneous for both of them, a term that would determine their joint existence, thus imagining their unity; in this manner, for example, the polar concepts of *matter* and *form* find their unity in a third concept — *thing* or *body;* the opposite concepts of stasis and change combine into the concept of life. Thus all conceivable definitions of idea possess a duality or are polar; moreover, idea itself in its reality is a third term that combines these corresponding or opposing attributes.

The activity of the mind is inherently limitless, since, insofar as its own property consists of the ability to reflect on itself, it can be compared with two mirrors placed opposite to each other and producing an endless series of reflections. According to the accurate expression of Schelling, the mind is a limitless potential of thought, and if it were to affirm itself in its exclusivity or egotism, its series of characteristics or particular ideas would process without end, never leading to the highest, final unity or genuine idea. But the original mind, with the force of its self-negation or as defined by divine Logos, presupposes the limit of its negative activity, and coordinating it with the will of absolute good and the perception of absolute

---

[a]. For this reason the philosophy of Hegel, for which our rational thought is absolute thought, knows idea only in the form of a concept.

beauty, brings its characteristics to the entire, absolute unity, which indeed is properly Truth or Idea as truth, since all particular ideas or truths are such, insofar as they represent necessary levels for the realization of the whole truth or the logical idea. Thus the logical development of a comprehensible idea is obedient to the general law of all development, according to which the detachment and differentiation of separate parts and elements that compose the second major stage of development do not continue endlessly (since in that case there would not be any kind of development, but only disintegration), but become a new, differentiated unity, which constitutes the goal of development.

If the characteristics of idea discernible to the mind composed an endless series, then the logical system of these characteristics evidently would be impossible. If, as is necessary, the entire series of logical characteristics converges into a certain higher unity in the idea itself, then we would not even have the need to know all the relative parts of this series (the number of which, although not limitless in actuality, may seem that way to our mind): it is sufficient for the logical system to reveal the most important of these relative characteristics, as well as the last and most important among the intermediate ones, as an embryologist studying the history of the development of a specific organism who has neither the possibility nor the need to point out all the stages of this development, but is satisfied to designate the most crucial ones. A logical system is a scheme of ideas, and therefore may designate *explicite* only the most important of its relative characteristics without any kind of damage to its general fullness and completeness, in a similar way to which a geographical scheme, i.e., a map, designates only the most important locations of a specific country, which in no wise prevents it from depicting the entire country.

The development of polar or relative characteristics of Idea forms the middle, most dialectical part of organic logic. Concerning the basic definitions under the categories of the existent, essence, and being that we examined in the preceding chapter, although they are cognized by the mind in its necessity and insofar as they are subject to logic, they are not produced by the mind, which is already clear from the fact that the mind itself is one of these attributes. They are produced by Logos as such prior to the mind and its conditions; therefore a magical, although secondary, cognition of them, it goes without saying, is conditioned by the mind.

Among the polar or relative characteristics, we will examine nine pairs under three categories: entity, organism, and person. In each pair of char-

Relative Categories That Define Idea as an Entity

acteristics their opposition is resolved in the third term, which properly is idea as the expression of truth: it is the synthesis that necessarily is preceded by thesis and antithesis — the form that from the distant past and out of necessity was adopted by every kind of dialectics. Thus we will examine only twenty-seven logical characteristics, and among them nine synthesizing ones, out of which each represents a certain particular truth; this last expresses the idea itself or the truth (κατεξοχήν).

Relative Characteristics of Idea as an Entity

The Same and the Other = Something

Every kind of thought consists of distinctions and combinations, and consequently presupposes formally three terms: two distinguishable ones and a third — their unity. Dialectical differentiation consists of the opposition of the one to the other. That, to which the other is opposed, or what is opposite to the other, is the same or itself (the identical one). In actuality, if the second term is the other while the first is distinguished from it, then it already is not the other; therefore, it is the same or the identical one. But since the opposition of terms is mutual, or reciprocal, so that if the second term is distinguished from the first and is its other, the first as well is distinguished from the second and is in exactly the same way the other for it, then consequently both of these properties belong indistinguishably to both terms and thus possess only a relative or subjective significance. But if the differentiated terms are the same and the other only relatively, in a reciprocal opposition, then what in fact are they irrelatively? If that, in which they are differentiated (the concept of the same and the other), possesses only a relative significance, then their irrelative defining property must be identical for them or express their unity. They necessarily must have such a property, because since those two categories (the same and the other) do not belong to the differentiated terms, but only to their differentiation, if they did not have a third property, they would be nothing in and of themselves. However, in such a case they could not even be differentiated, could not find themselves in a position of interrelationship, since nothing cannot be differentiated from nothing, nothing cannot be placed in any kind of relationship with nothing. Thus, if difference is conceived (and it is conceived in the relative concepts of *the same* and *the other*), then what ought to be conceived as well is something discernible; the differentiated terms in any case must be something, each of them equally must be *something*. Thus we find in the concept *something* the characteristic that constitutes the objective content, and along with it the unity of the first two discernible terms.

If *something* is equally the content of *the same* and *the other*, then the question arises: How are these three terms distinguishable from each other? If all three terms are something, then the third term is something as such, while the first two are something in their self-differentiation. Thus the third, synthetic term is in essence the first, while the two remaining ones are only its corollaries. But to understand this self-differentiation of the first idea as anything at all, we must point out the specific basis of the differentiation. If the logical content or essence (Idea) of the three terms is identical, since all of them equally are nothing, then what are the details of their particular content that make them differentiated? In not possessing its own foundation in general logical content or logical form, it [the essence] may consist only of the mode of being. Only three modes of being are conceivable: *being as the unmediated manifestation of the existent, being of itself or will; being as the reflected manifestation of the existent, being for itself or imagination; and being as the state of the existent, defined in reverse by its imagination, being in itself or feeling.* Moreover, it is evident that the third mode of being is the unity or synthesis of the first two. In the first mode being is identical with the existent, is its own spontaneous manifestation — will; in the second it is distinguished from the existent, is considered as its other; in the third the distinction again is eliminated in a synthetic unity. From here it is clear that the definition of the same, or identity, corresponds to the first mode; the definition of the other, or differentiation, to the second; and the definition of their unity, or something, to the third. In this way we have deduced for our three terms the necessary characteristics for their differentiation. All three are something, but the first is something as an object or the content of the will (in being existing of itself), the second is something as an object or the content of the imagination (in being existing for itself), and the third is something as an object or the content of feeling (in being existing in itself). In other words, something is the same, insofar as it is desired or affirmed by the will; it is the other, insofar as it is imagined; and it is the unity of the same and the other or properly something, insofar as it is felt; and since we know that to each mode of being there corresponds a particular object or form of the existent, our logical terms are strengthened by these objects and thus are *real-*

Relative Categories That Define Idea as an Entity

ized or made manifest. On the other hand, these objects themselves, and consequently their unity as well or idea, receive in these three logical categories (the same, the other, and something) their first general logical content and thus are *generalized*.

It is understandable that if something is actually desired, imagined, and felt, this something inherently, by its existence or substantially, is distinguished from its being for other subjects in the form of will, imagination, and feeling; in other words, idea (since *something* is only the first logical definition of idea) inherently is distinguished from its being for spirit, mind, and soul. And although in this last (soul), idea is affirmed as such and consequently receives its actual realization, this realization of the idea in the soul and the idea itself, however, are identical only in content or essence *(essentia)*, and not substantially or in existence *(existentia)*, since in reality the soul could not also make manifest the idea or affirm it as such, if the idea did not first exist in and of itself.

Thus by the substantial content or particular existence we have four terms, while by the logical content or form, only three. This situation — that our four substantial elements represent in a logical relationship merely a threefold differentiation — derives from the relative character of purely logical definitions. In actuality, although from the objective point of view, i.e., for idea, a certain logical definition corresponds only to one specific mode of being and one specific object (precisely the definition of the same corresponds to will and spirit; the definition of the other, to imagination and mind; their logical unity or something corresponds to feeling and soul, and hence idea itself as a substantial unity is no longer the third but the fourth term), for these objects themselves such an exclusive correspondence cannot exist, since each of them equally for itself is the same or itself (because nothing cannot be an other for its own self, but necessarily is for itself the same). Consequently, the two remaining ones are for it equally as others; i.e., both together are subject to the logical definition of *the other*. Hence any of the objects represents the first logical term, or the same (itself); the two others, the second logical term, or the other; and their internal unity or Idea is thus the third, not the fourth, term. On the other hand, since every kind of real (and not purely logical or relative) definition must be at least two-sided,[b] and consequently presupposes one that is defined,

---

b. Since in a one-sided definition, i.e., in the light solely of that which is defining, what is defined would be completely obscured by this sole definer; as a result, what is defined

PRINCIPLES OF ORGANIC LOGIC (CONTINUATION)

two that are defining, and over and above this, their unity as the basis or medium[1] of the definition, there necessarily emerge four substantial elements situated within a threefold logical relationship.

We found in the concept of *something* the first logical definition of Idea. This concept, just like those from which it derives (the same and the other), possesses such a general and indefinite meaning that our construction of it may seem an empty word game. But the essence of the dialectics, which is the proper method of organic logic, consists of the fact that the thinking mind, considering the most general and indefinite concept, by means of consistent acts of thought, develops the content of this concept, which is found in it at first only potentially, in these same acts of thought receiving its definite reality. And this is the only possible method in the first or fundamental branch of philosophy; since the task of philosophy generally consists of the reasonable explanation of every specific, real content, i.e., in its logically conceived construction or deduction, philosophy cannot at first be based on this real content that it must still deduce; consequently it must begin only with such concepts that do not yet possess a definite content and reality and that are only purely conceived potentials or possibilities. Concrete reality is the *task* of philosophy, and in no wise the principle or *origin* of it. For this reason, even the concept *something*, with all its common accessibility, cannot serve as the point of departure for logic, since it already possesses a certain, albeit scanty, specificity — insofar as something is not nothing. Indisputably the first principle of logic, and consequently of all of philosophy, may be only the concept of the absolute or superexistent, with which we in fact began our exposition. The absolute is not even something: it is the potential unity (indifferentness, identity) of nothing and something, and hence no longer has any specificity.

All systems of speculative philosophy that are to any extent consistent acknowledge in expressions of one sort or another the concept of the absolute as their first principle. Moreover, these systems to the greatest extent confuse the concept of the absolute with the concept of being in general — and this is far from being the same thing, since being in general is already a certain definition, insofar as it is opposed to nonbeing. And furthermore,

---

would not be differentiated from the definer, i.e., in this case what is defined would not be present at all, and when the defined is absent, that which is defining is absent as well. Thus a one-sided definition, i.e., a definition only by means of that which is defining, destroys its own self, and therefore is logically impossible.

the majority of these systems, starting from the teaching of the Hellene Parmenides and ending with the *Identitätsphilosophie*[2] of Schelling, in acknowledging in fairness the concept of the absolute as the *origin* of philosophy, also mistakenly accept this concept in the same indefiniteness or potentiality as the *end* of philosophy, as a consequence of which all their philosophizing necessarily relates to the simple affirmation of this indifferent absolute (or absolute indifference) in opposition to every definite reality, i.e., to the simple negation of this last. Genuine philosophy, or integral knowledge, in deriving from the concept of absolute potential, supposes as the end or final result of philosophy the absolute as well, but already *realized*, i.e., in its complete specificity and entire reality, it being known that philosophy itself is the organic development of the original conception of the absolute, as the indefinite potential in its real wholly definite idea. Thus, here as well the absolute emerges as the beginning and end, the alpha and omega of philosophy, but in a different sense: the first conception of the absolute and its final idea relate to each other as the seed of a plant to the very same plant, completely developed and fertile; academic philosophy is content with a single seed of truth, having dried it up with abstract formulas.

If idea in general is the specificity of the absolute, it is understandable that already the first logical expression of the idea of *something*, for all its impoverishment, at least represents some sort of definition. Idea is something — in this is contained the necessity of further development. If idea is something, however, then what can it be? In actuality, it is impossible to be something or anything in general, since in the very concept *something* or *anything* are contained the negation of its generality and the requirement of definite, particular content, which are not yet given in this concept itself. When I say *anything*, I presuppose something definite, although I do not indicate in this concept *what in particular*. Thus the indefiniteness of the concept *something* or *anything* is relative and, so to speak, preliminary, requiring its elimination. And so, what does this primary something consist of? What is the subsequent content of the essential idea, and in it of the superexistent absolute? The gradual answer to this question is the entire subsequent exposition. But before we turn to the development of further definitions of Idea, it is necessary to make the following four observations regarding what has already been stated.

First. All relative definitions are already contained *implicite* in those primary definitions, which under the name of basic definitions constituted the subject of the previous chapter; they were contained in them specifically as their relationships, and examining now especially these relative definitions, we only consider them *explicite*. We encountered them already during the exposition of the first principles, but at that time we did not focus our attention on them, because they were not the proper subject or goal of our exposition; now we are making them precisely such a goal, and this corresponds perfectly with the general law of organic development, according to which no element or defining form of an organism is created anew, but only those that already existed in the bud. In other words, in the course of development particular elements or parts of an organism, being originally absorbed and not separated, individually become a particular goal, so that it is possible to state that development consists of the fact that the organizational force of life gradually concentrates its attention and its action on separate elements, in order to subsequently bring them together into a new unity. It goes without saying that in the development of logical definitions the role of this organizational force is played by the cognizing mind. Such a derivation of logical categories, in the light of which each one would appear instantly and for the first time in its dialectical place, arising directly out of the preceding one — must be acknowledged as completely impossible. The original mind, brought about by absolute Logos, conceives of relative definitions, but since this pure activity of the original mind cannot be subject to time, but is consequently eternal in the positive and unconditional meaning of this term, all these definitions exist eternally in common with each other, and equally as well with the basic principles of the existent, essence, and being, and all of them are in mutual interaction, defining each other. For this reason it is impossible to examine the basic definitions in unconditional separateness from the relative ones, and vice versa. At any rate, even in the absolute, logical definitions do not arise out of one another, but rather all of them similarly come from Logos itself by means of the original mind. Our mind does not produce them, neither as one from the other, nor from out of its own self, but on the contrary, it itself in its logical activity is determined by these definitions as already givens independent of it, and for this reason only reproduces them by its thought process in their normal correlation and unity, or, as indicated, organizes them for itself.

Second. Every act of purely logical thinking, consisting of discernment and combination, refers as to its primary form to the law of identity, i.e., $A = A$. Here, evidently emphasizing the identity of the first and second A, we by means of the same emphasize their difference as well, since without the last the first would be impossible. In actuality, since it is possible to compare and identify among themselves only a few, at least two different objects, in comparing and identifying A with its own self, by means of the same we divide it into two, i.e., distinguish it from its own self or understand it as an other to its own self or for itself. Along with this, in this very contradiction we are convinced of its formal identity with its own self, since the other A does not possess any other content, in no way differs formally from the first, is the same A, only instantiated another time, i.e., the difference between them does not concern their content of essence, but only the act of their affirmation or existence; in other words, this difference is only a numerical one. Thus the basic logical law or general form of thought expresses the unity of the one and the other or of identity and difference, but not in one and the same relationship, which would be a contradiction, but rather in various respects, specifically identity in its essence or content and difference in its existence or the act of affirmation. The law of identity either does not have any meaning (this is how it is usually understood in formal logic), or has the following connotation: that same, which is divided in half or is distinguished from its own self *by the existence* or *act of its affirmation,* and along with this is identical with itself or one *in its essence* or *content*. Only in this sense does the understood law of identity become productive and receive a defining significance not only for logic but also for all of philosophy.

In the light of the above, however, it is necessary to keep in mind the following distinction. For us, insofar as we exist in time, the distinction of anything at all by its existence or its act of affirmation may relate to a simple distinction in time or in a moment of affirmation. Thus when we state $A = A$, the difference between the second and the first A consists only in the fact that they are conceived by us as two distinct moments of time, one following the other, since it is impossible in one moment of time, in one temporal act, to conceive of A in two positions or to imagine two times that this is A. Thus the entire necessary distinction by existence between them refers to the fact that the second A exists in another moment of time than the first, or that the act by which we conceive of the second A is numerically different from the one by which we conceive of the first — only numerically another, since in everything that remains these two acts are identical; i.e., not only do they possess one and the same content, specifically A, but the very *mode* of their existence, or the mode by which they affirm their content, is completely identical, insofar as both are the identical acts of one and the same purely logical thought. But if here a difference of existence refers to a difference of time, this is inconceivable in the application to the original activity, which cannot be subject to time, of the most absolute Logos. Consequently, in it the difference by existence has to do with the mode of existence itself, i.e., this difference lies not in the fact that one and the same content is assumed in various moments of time, but in the fact that *one and the same content in diverse ways is assumed or affirmed*, to wit: first, as what is imagined; second, as what is desired; and third, as what is felt. Only as a result of such threefold-ness of *modi*, and consequently, of the subjects as well in the light of the identicalness of content, is possible a joint affirmation without any discernment of time, i.e., affirmation in a single moment or, what is the same, in a single eternity. For this reason, when the original mind conceives of some sort of difference, the real basis of this difference lies not in conception or thought, but in will or feeling; the conception provides only the form of the difference. In this are contained the indissoluble bond and unsolvable knot that combine three modes of being among themselves and through them as well the three subjects corresponding to the three *modi*.

Third. In the definition of the same and the other, *implicite* and directly, are contained several other characteristics that can be directly extracted from them. Concerning these characteristics, both the polar and correlative ones, as has been examined above, we consider it necessary to focus especially on two of them. The first is *the one* and *the many*. The same or itself as such is the one, while in the distinction or supposition of the other multiplicity is assumed. In other words, in distinguishing or imagining itself as an other it multiplies, and consequently their unity is the unity of the one and the many. Since only the many can differentiate itself (since the one, in differentiating itself, in distinguishing itself, becomes the many, or multiplies without ceasing to be the one by virtue of the general law of every kind of action, and thus combining in itself the substantial unity with the phenomenal multiplicity), and on the other hand the multiplicity may be present only upon the *discernment* of many (by virtue of the law of *identitatis indiscernibilium*),[3] it follows that these two characteristics are only two expressions or two subjective sides of one and the same concept. The other correlative characteristic that flows out of our first definition is *unconditional* and *relative*. We call "unconditional" that which is not defined by anything else, and does not possess externally to it-

Relative Categories That Define Idea as an Entity

self anything else as a condition of its being. Thus the identical one as such or in and of itself is unconditional, distinguishing or assuming an other, to which it relates and through which it becomes relative. It is evident that when two things relate to each other, they must first of all be outside a relationship, i.e., unconditional, because if they were nothing or were not by means of nothing outside a relationship, i.e., in and of themselves or unconditional, then their relationship would be the relationship of nothing to nothing, i.e., it would not exist at all, since it is not possible for nothing to relate to nothing. Thus, by means of this same, that something is relative, it is unconditional as well, or *everything relative is unconditional*. But exactly in the same way *everything unconditional is necessarily relative*, since it, in differentiating itself from the relative as the other, by this same finds itself in a relationship with it, i.e., is itself relative. In reality, when we think of the unconditional, in this concept inherently there is no positive content; as the negative form of this term already demonstrates, by "unconditional" is understood only the absence of that which we call "conditional" or "relative"; in this is exhausted the entire purely logical content of this concept, which thus possesses a completely negative meaning. As a logical concept, the unconditional, i.e., *unconditionality*, is wholly defined by its opposite, and consequently itself is completely conditional or relative, thus representing the direct negation of its own definition. But in the face of this kind of dialectic, in which concepts turn out to be directly opposite to themselves, what happens to the law of identity? The kind of philosophy that examines general logical definitions not as predicates of the existent or existents, but as pure abstract forms inherently independent in their abstractness, for which thus everything is exhausted by means of purely logical, formal content or the general form of these definitions, so that for it [this philosophy] there do not properly exist *the unconditional, the one, the various*, etc., but only *unconditionality, unity, difference*, etc. — this kind of purely formal philosophy, being consistent, necessarily must negate the law of identity, which fact we indeed find in the representative of this philosophy — in Hegel. Here we must once again focus our attention on the essential difference of organic logic from the logic of Hegel.

This is the *fourth* observation, in which, incidentally, I will confine myself to only a few comments, since it would be more reasonable to provide a comprehensive parallel between Hegelian logic and organic logic after an exposition of this last. Since for Hegel truth is presented only from its formal side, from the side of pure thought, then for him all logical definitions are not predicates of the existent or existents, but rather are affirmed in and of themselves in their abstractness, so that, for example, the definition of the self or the same for him is only a general concept of selfness or identity, while the definition of the other exists only as the general concept "to be an other," i.e., the concept of other-being or difference. Consequently, according to Hegel, the identity of the same and the other is the identity of identity and difference, or to put it differently — the identity of itself and its opposite. And in actuality, this affirmation that the absolute idea in its most general form is the identity of identity and difference or of itself and its opposite constitutes the basic position of all Hegelian logic, and consequently of all his philosophy as well. For some people this paradoxical position is (or, to put it better, was, since nowadays one will scarcely find pure Hegelians in the entire world, which, it goes without saying, does not prevent Hegelianism both now and in the future to exert an enormous influence on philosophy and science) the highest formula of the most absolute truth; for other people this paradoxical position is simply an absurdity, and the entire philosophy of Hegel, which is based on this absurdity, is the raving of a madman or the blatant nonsense of a charlatan (such, as is well known, was the opinion of the famous Schopenhauer); in reality this is only the one-sided, and moreover the negative, expression of truth, affirmed as its absolute and positive expression and in this sense undoubtedly false. We saw in actuality and will see even more later that purely logical categories have a relative and dialectical character. Each of them, taken in its separateness or abstractness, is transformed into its opposite, thus turning out to be untruthful in this form, and consequently their truth or ideal is contained in their unity. But this unity is inconceivable without differences (since that which does not differ also cannot combine), and since such differences do not exist in these categories in and of themselves or when examined abstractly because in this form they are transformed into each other, the necessary difference may appear, only insofar as these categories are the actual relationships of several existents or, grammatically speaking, the predicates of several subjects. Thus these purely logical categories as relative presuppose other basic or substantial categories, with which we began our exposition.

We know that logical categories as imagined in thought are not primary, because thought presupposes a thinker, while a thinker presupposes someone who wills and someone who feels. The thinking mind in the definition of selfness or identity imagines, evidently, his own self for himself, while in the definition of an other imagines a willing spirit and feeling soul as conceivable or for him and through this brings them forth in this quality, since, although they are in and of themselves, as what is conceivable, they can be imagined only by the mind. Thus if the primary subjects really differ by means of logical categories, this difference does not depend exclusively either on the existents themselves or on logical *categories* in and of themselves. Since in reality logical *categories* (the same and the other, the one and the many, the unconditional and the relative, etc.) express, it is evident, several relationships, but a relationship necessarily requires those who relate (since without this it becomes an empty word), while on the other hand, those who relate as such require a certain means or form of relationship, it follows that logical *categories* receive their reality from the existents, while the existents receive their form or specificity from the logical concepts. But this is not the case for Hegel, who does not acknowledge anything except purely logical or relative categories, and his philosophy begins directly from them.[c] He is unable to conceive of the existent or existents, since his first principle is the pure abstracted being or the concept *an sich*. The subject represents for him only one of the succeeding moments in the self-development of the pure concept, as one of the forms of logical being, and not as the existent. For this reason, for him all logical categories are predicates without subjects, relationships without those who relate. In such a form they lose all actual specificity, become fluid: each of them without hindrance is transformed into its opposite, and the establishment of this identity or undifferentiation of opposing categories, taken in their abstraction, or the indication of their fluidity constitutes the entire essence of Hegelian dialectics. If for us the circumstance that logical categories in and of themselves, in an abstracted form (i.e., without any substantial content or as predicates without subjects), are transformed one into the other and thus contradict the law of identity — if this circumstance, I say, proves to us the falseness of that abstracted form, then Hegel, on the contrary, in acknowledging this abstracted form as absolute truth, from the indicated contradiction, draws a

c. Hegel understands *being*, from which he begins his logic, not as the means or *modus* of the self-orientation of the superexistent (according to which meaning, being is one of the basic and positive categories), but only as the general concept of being, abstracted from all features and not belonging to any subject; in this sense being possesses, evidently, a purely relative and completely negative character, as a consequence of which it becomes equivalent to the concept of *nothing*.

conclusion only concerning the falseness of the law of identity; hence it is clear that the negation of this law on the part of Hegel constitutes only a necessary consequence of that principle of abstract rationalism or formalism, of which this philosopher is the most prominent and most consistent representative, such that from this negative standpoint as well Hegel's philosophy is significant as a brilliant *reductio ad absurdum*[4] of an entire philosophical current in its exclusivity.

Definition of Causes and Effects: Their Unity or Reality: The Thing-in-Itself and Phenomenon

We have established the difference between the same and the other. A distinguishes B from itself as its other. Insofar as A distinguishes from itself what is its other, insofar as this last exists for it, it evidently has an understanding of this other. If I distinguish something from myself or place something before myself as an object, in this distinction or in the quality of my representation this object has an understanding of me. Every object as something that exists for a subject, or as its representation, is evidently an effect of the subject itself. Thus B, insofar as A distinguishes it from itself, or imagines it as its other, is the circumstance or *effect* of this same A, and consequently A is its *cause*. In other words, the same or itself is the cause of its other as such.

This is one aspect of the matter, and that philosophy (subjective idealism) that is limited by this aspect, or accepts one-sided truth as the whole truth, necessarily arrives at the kinds of conclusions that not only find themselves in a powerless contradiction with reality, but are logically inconceivable as well. In reality, the other cannot be only the effect of the self; an object cannot be only the product of a subject. As a consequence of the relativity of these concepts, itself or the same is conceivable only in relation to an other, and consequently it as such presupposes an other or is defined by it. In this sense it itself is as much the effect of its other as the other is its effect. In general the cause as such is only the cause of effect, and without it the cause does not exist. Consequently, the cause as such depends on its effect and is defined by it; in other words, the effect is the cause of its own cause, or the cause is the effect of its own effect. Thus, in abstract terms there is, properly speaking, neither a cause nor an effect; the logical distinction between them in this kind of abstraction turns out to be

Relative Categories That Define Idea as an Entity

illusive. But it acquires this real meaning if we examine these concepts in their truthful sense, i.e., as predicates of certain subjects.

As we have seen, that which for a certain subject as the same or itself is only its other, and thus itself in and of itself, is the same kind of subject as the first, which for it likewise is an other. If the other were designated for us as an effect, and the same as the cause, we must say that something, being an effect with respect to a certain subject, in and of itself constitutes the same kind of cause as that subject or, to put it more precisely, has its particular cause that is independent of this subject. Thus the other is not exclusively either an effect of the first subject as such or its cause. It is both the one and the other, but in different respects. As existing for this subject it is its effect, but it could not exist for it, i.e., this subject could not imagine it, if it itself were not defined by the other — not by the other as this effect, which as such does not exist ahead of this subject, but rather by the other as its own cause of this effect, i.e., another subject. Thus an other existing for a certain subject is neither, properly speaking, an effect or a cause, but the interaction between this and another subject. Every effect thus constitutes the interaction of two subjects and necessarily has at least two causes.

From the aforementioned it is clear that the original subjects find their connection or unity not in the concepts of cause and effect, it being the case that between them there would be a one-sided subordination, but only in the concept of interaction or reality, in the light of which they retain their independence. Thus in this category idea or truth is defined as the interaction of basic subjects, which in this interaction differ by means of the relative categories of cause and effect. This interaction of basic subjects is their *reality*. A nonacting cause, evidently, does not possess reality, but receives it only through its own effect; every effect of the cause is its [the cause's] interaction with another [cause], since it is impossible to act upon nothing or in a state of nothingness. Thus the basic subjects in and of themselves, in their separateness or abstracted from each other, are only potentials, do not possess reality, and acquire it only in their interaction, i.e., in idea. Thus, idea is their reality. Connecting this definition with what we learned in the previous category, we find that idea is *something real* or *a certain reality*.

From the categories of cause and effect directly are derived the categories *thing-in-itself* and *phenomenon*. We call "phenomenon" every effect that exists for us or is apparent to us (hence "appearance," φαινόμενον — from φαίνεσθαι), an effect that is predicated, on the one hand, on a perceiving subject, and on the other, on a certain producing cause independent of the perceiving subject, a cause that as such cannot be immediately apparent but is revealed only in its effect or phenomenon; independently of it [the effect] we attribute to this cause one's own in-itself being and call it "in-itself existent," "self-existent," or "thing-in-itself" — *Ding an sich*.[d] Thus phenomenon is the effect of the thing-in-itself, and the thing-in-itself is the personal or producing cause of the phenomenon. This is because if one understands phenomena in the sense of subjective idealism, i.e., as purely ideal manifestations of a creatively thinking subject, then the material character of these manifestations, which in fact is peculiar to them, may depend only on the fact that the subject is called forth or defined in opposition to the production of these manifestations or phenomena by something independent of it that possesses the significance of a material-producing cause of these phenomena (only the significance of the formal cause always belongs to the subject). This is allowed not only by Kant in his *Ding an sich*, but also by Fichte in his absolute *Schranke*,[5] the same as by Berkeley in his concept of Divinity that evokes ideas in us.

In returning to the concepts of "in-itself being" and "phenomenon" as purely logical categories, we can easily see that they have meaning only as the predicates of certain subjects; moreover, both of them can belong to one and the same subject in different respects, and not only can, but must. The in-itself existent subject necessarily also contains other-being or phenomenon, since the concept in-*itself* presupposes the discernment of the self as different from an other; as a result, there arises the relationship to this last or the effect on it, i.e., phenomenon. On the other hand, the phenomenon, i.e., being for an other, presupposes the one that exists for the other; a phenomenon presupposes that which appears, which already aside from this relationship cannot itself be a phenomenon, and consequently is the in-itself existent or the thing-in-itself.

It is likewise clear, and I have already pointed this out more than once, that being for an other or phenomenon coincides with the form of cognition in general, so this form by its very definition cannot be anything other than a phenomenon. If in actuality to be a phenomenon according to the

---

d. I retain the term "thing-in-itself" as a literal translation of *Ding an sich* not because I considered this term of Kant entirely precise and adequate, but because it has entered universal usage in philosophy and it would be awkward from a practical standpoint to replace it with another.

logical sense means only to exist for an other, and if exactly in the same way to be cognized according to the logical sense means only to exist for an other, then it is evident that these two concepts, as wholly covered by a third one, are equal to each other. But since, on the other hand, a phenomenon is impossible without that which appears, then every kind of cognition, being formally a phenomenon, relates to that which appears or the existent-in-itself, which thus, as never being able to be entirely transformed into the form of cognition, insofar as that which appears cannot coincide with the phenomenon, is in this sense uncognized and also is solely cognized, insofar as every kind of cognition relates to it as to its substantial content, and that about which the given content is cognized, about which the given predicates or attributes are affirmed, is precisely this existent. As every kind of my cognition about you is undoubtedly a phenomenon, you yourselves, about whom I am thinking this and whom I conceive in this, no longer constitute a phenomenon, but rather that which appears, which becomes for me as an other, produces this cognition in me, and in it is cognized by me.

If according to the concept itself, every kind of phenomenon is a phenomenon of the existent or the thing-in-itself, in exactly the same way and in every kind of cognition something about this existent is cognized, and from the fact that the existent-in-itself as such can never take on the form of cognition, i.e., itself become cognition, it is evident that it does not follow for it [cognition] to be unconditionally uncognizable, since to be cognition and to be cognized are two completely different concepts.

As a result of the abstract character of academic philosophy, which isolates logical concepts and affirms them in such exclusivity, academic philosophers did not acknowledge and to this day do not acknowledge the necessary cognizability (in the sense of the word explained above) of the in-itself existent, not taking into account the simplicity and clarity of this truth, while one of the greatest of these philosophers, Kant, insists with particular harshness on the opposition between the existent-in-itself, *Ding an sich,* and the world of phenomena as two unconditionally separate and incompatible spheres. According to his assertion, the circumstance that we formally cognize only phenomena makes it impossible for us to cognize the thing-in-itself; in reality it is possible with equal legitimacy to assert that, just as we cognize only phenomena, so we cognize only the thing-in-itself — this depends on the meaning of the word "cognize." Moreover, it is evident that one cannot arbitrarily take one of these meanings when both are equally necessary and not only are entirely compatible but also logically presuppose one another. Many important mistakes in philosophy originate from a simple inaccuracy in the formulation of logical questions. If Kant had completely and clearly defined the logical relationship between the concepts of phenomenon and thing-in-itself, and likewise between the concepts "cognized" and "cognizable," instead of limiting himself on this point to indefinite and figurative expressions, he would very likely have avoided the error that turned out to be of this kind for his philosophy and led to its self-decay. Already Fichte, and subsequently Schelling and Hegel, decisively rejected the unconditional opposition between *Ding an sich* and phenomenon, although they, especially the last, as we will now see, fell into the opposite extreme. At the same time, however, in more superficial philosophy, which ignores everything that in Kant was truthful and sublime — his transcendental aesthetics, i.e., his doctrine about the ideal character of forms of space and time, and his doctrine about the distinction between the empirical and speculative character and about the combination of transcendental freedom with phenomenological necessity — in this, I say, superficial philosophy, which is not capable of assessing and therefore ignores "these finest diamonds in the philosophical crown of Kant," the indicated error of this great thinker was made into a trivial fable that started being promulgated by such quasi philosophers who, while not possessing the merits of Kant, should at least have avoided his mistakes.

In serious philosophy the alogical division, or unconditional dualism between *Ding an sich* and phenomenon, was once and for all eliminated by Hegel; but he, as has been noted, assumed the opposite extreme and identified phenomenon with that which appears, which, properly speaking, leads to the negation of this last. In particular, the second part of Hegel's logic — *über das Wesen* — is devoted to the development of this view. The basis for this new error — a new one, incidentally, only in European philosophy, since in India over the course of slightly more than two thousand years before Hegel the philosophers of Buddhism carried out such an identification of the existent with phenomenon, or the negation of every existent, with much greater consistency and boldness than Hegel himself — is contained in the most general principle of Hegelian philosophy, according to which he did not acknowledge any real and primary subject of logical predicates or attributes, but took these attributes in and of themselves in their generality or abstraction. But the in-itself existent is precisely the constant subject of phenomena, and consequently could not be allowed by Hegel as something real, but rather appears in his writing as only one of the limited reflexive concepts, eliminated in the abstract dialectical process.

What is truthful in the view of Hegel remains, undoubtedly, only the fact that the categories of *Ding an sich* and phenomenon possess a relative character, not an unconditional one, as Kant imagined. As a consequence of this relativity, one cannot say simply that a certain a or x is in-itself existent, or a thing-in-itself, while a certain b or y is a phenomenon; since every a and b, x and y is necessarily at one and the same time both the in-itself existent and the phenomenon, only in different respects and to differing degrees. For the same reason, it cannot be said that metaphysical philosophy has as its subject only essences or things-in-themselves, while positive science examines only phenomena, since in that case both metaphysics and science would have as their subject something nonexistent and even logically impossible. In actuality both of these branches of human knowledge have as their subject *the existent as it appears*, or in phenomena they cognize something about the existent that is revealed in phenomena. Consequently, between them there is not and cannot be an unconditional and fundamental contradiction; instead, there exists only a relative and graded distinction, insofar as science cognizes the existent primarily in absolute or conditional phenomena or effects; metaphysics cognizes it [the existent] in original or conditioning phenomena — in other words, in defining causes.

As a matter of fact, there exists neither the thing-in-itself nor the phenomenon, but rather a single absolutely-existent, which is both the alpha and omega, the one and the everything, the beginning and the end, which in its completeness contains both absolute-being-in-itself and the origin of all phenomena; all the remaining entities and forms of existence are represented only through the various degrees of its self-position or manifestation. We will understand this better when we discuss the integral characteristics of the idea. At this point I will observe that only with the correct view of the relative character of the concepts of being-in-itself and phenomenon-in-itself as different but not divided, and combined but not blended, is it possible to understand faithfully and satisfactorily other special relationships in the sphere of metaphysics, as for example, the relationship of divinity to the world, of the spirit to nature, of the soul to the body — an absence of this understanding necessarily leads either to indifferent monism and monologism, in which all categories disappear and what results is a dialectical fog, where any category can be taken for any other, as in the French saying *la nuit tous les chats sout gris*,[6] or to that limited dualism, which, in dividing unconditionally the first principles of being, transforms the world and nature into a lifeless machine, and turns divinity and spirit into some kind of impotent phantoms.

Definitions of Matter and Form

All effects perceived by the imagining mind or all phenomena that take place in it as its internal states necessarily receive its own definitions or are defined by its own nature. Thus the imagining mind necessarily provides the *form* of the phenomena, since it is evident that something may exist for it and in it only in the form of its own being. That which is subject to this form, i.e., the things or subjects acting on it, constitute by these same the *matter* of phenomena, and if, as we have stated, every effect or phenomenon presupposes two at least mutually interactive causes, then one of them — the perceiving subject or mind — is the formal cause while the other — that which acts on it — is the material cause.

But if the imagining mind may imagine and act only according to the definition of its own nature or being, and consequently provide the necessary form to all phenomena that exist for it, then exactly the same thing must evidently be said about other subjects as well. The spirit and soul in exactly the same way must perceive and act only according to the definitions of their own nature; in this sense they likewise provide a form for phenomena, and for them the mind must be only a material cause. Hence each of the subjects for itself is a form, while the others for it represent only matter. In this respect, thus, different subjects exclude each other; they cannot have their unity in the definition of form as subjective, exclusively belonging to each of them. Consequently, they may possess their necessary unity only in a certain general objective form. This form cannot constitute a single one of the three subjects as such or taken separately, since as such they possess only a subjective, exclusive form that does not present any basis for objective unity; consequently, they may have the necessary general form only in that which for all of them is general and objective in the same way, i.e., in the idea.

Thus, the idea is the form. But if it were only the form, and consequently would have its matter not in its own self but in three subjects, then it could not be their real and objective unity. In reality, we would obviously have circular logic: on the one hand, the three subjects must have possessed their unity in the idea as the form; on the other hand, this very idea as only form is consequently deprived of any kind of personal content or matter, it could be defined only as the general unity of the subjects, and thus we could not go further than the tautology that the unity of subjects lies in their unity. It is not in doubt that every kind of unity is possible only under a general form of unity, but it is equally indisputable that this form alone is insufficient. To be valid, the principle of unity must possess a particular positive content or matter. I will clarify this with a concrete example.

Many highly respected people, incidentally, being distressed at the prevailing anarchy of minds in our day, as a means to counteract it and as a unifying principle of humankind, point to what they call "social ideals." It would be pointless to search for a meaning in these words, to presuppose in them some kind of definite content: in these words is expressed only the formal requirement of the unifying principle in general in the guise of abstract concepts of community, brotherhood, a common goal, etc. Thus, in answer to the question, "What can internally unify society?" people answer, "Social ideals," and in answer to the question, "What, then, do social ideals consist of?" they answer, "They consist of the internal unity of society," not suspecting that they are not moving from the position of circular logic. Meanwhile, here it is already completely evident that a general abstract concept of social unity (which, of course, does not gain anything from the fact that it is adorned with the prestigious term "ideal"), in being deprived of any positive content, cannot bring about any kind of action. To unify humankind in spite of the completely real and mighty force of egotism, which divides people, is a task that is difficult and for the gods, but to accomplish it by means of abstract ideals, i.e., properly speaking, of an understanding of the ideal, is just as impossible as using a cardboard cannon to break through a stone wall. In reality, when different people and society became unified internally, on the basis of this unity or through this unifying and connecting principle, there appeared, not abstract ideas or ideals, but positive religions possessing a definite content (which perhaps acquired their name from this connecting force peculiar to them: *religio* — from *religiare*). If even to this day the religious, i.e., connecting content existing in humankind, were to turn out to be insufficient, it does not at all follow from this according to sensible reasoning that one must reject any positive content, but only that the old content should be replaced by that

PRINCIPLES OF ORGANIC LOGIC (CONTINUATION)

which is new or reformulated. Those who cannot suggest such a new content or even in principle reject in advance every religious, i.e., connecting, principle would perform a better service if they did not complain about the mental anarchy and did not offer in the capacity of connecting principles the kind of trifle with which, according to the German expression, one could not lure a dog out from behind a stove.

But let us return to our definitions. We found that an idea cannot be only a form possessing its matter or content in something else, but that it consequently in itself should have its matter and thus be just as much matter as it is form, i.e., the unity of the one and the other. Thus an idea is the unity or synthesis of matter and form. Only by means of this synthesis is a *definite existence* or *reality* formed. Every kind of reality consists of a specific combination of matter and form. Thus, an idea as the unity of matter and form is reality and a definite existence.[e] In combining this new definition with the preceding ones, we arrive at the situation that *an idea is something that actually and definitely exists*, or is *a certain actual reality*, or to describe these concepts in one word, *an idea is an entity*.

Note: Between the concepts of "actuality" and "reality" there exists a logically clear, though empirically always relative, distinction. Something possessing an internal actuality cannot be realized, and as a consequence cannot possess reality. The creative idea of an artist possesses actuality but is deprived of reality until it is realized in external material. Actuality and reality relate to each other as producing and produced, as *natura naturans* and *natura naturata*. Despite this clear, logical distinction between the two concepts, not all new languages have two words for their designation. Whereas in Russian and German, besides the words реальность and *Realität*, which they have in common with the French *réalité* and the English "reality," originating from the same source, Latin, there exists a specific fundamental word действительность, *Wirklichkeit*, hence both of these related but different concepts possess a specific corresponding expression — in French and English, on the contrary, one word designating reality serves as well for the designation of actuality, and thus in these languages both concepts have the same identity, or properly speaking, the

---

e. Form without matter possesses a general specificity, but does not have its own existence. Matter without form possesses existence as potential or form, but does not have any specificity. The combination of them possesses both the one and the other and is, in this manner, a definite existence or reality.

Relative Categories That Define Idea as an Entity

concept of actuality disappears, being swallowed by the concept of reality.[f] In the light of their language, the French and the English can acknowledge only a realized, material reality, since for the expression of an unreal actuality proper they do not have a word. This corresponds to the tendency of these peoples to attach significance only to that which is realized in firm, definite forms. Whether or not in this case a deficiency of language[g] affected the character of popular consciousness, or, to the contrary, the realism of the popular character is expressed by the absence of words for more spiritual concepts, since the popular mind creates language for itself in its own image and likeness, at any rate this circumstance is very typical. The identification of existence in general with material existence or the exclusive acknowledgment of this last and the negation of every kind of material reality has been expressed in English especially sharply in the fact that for the concept ничто, *nichts,* in this language the word "nothing" is used, which, properly speaking, signifies "not a thing" or "not any kind of thing," and similarly for the concept нечто or что-нибудь, *etwas,* the word "something," i.e., некотора вещь, is used. Thus, according to the meaning of this language, only material being, only a thing, is something, for otherwise what is not a thing by this same would be nothing: "what is not thing is nothing, of course" [these words appear in English in the original]. With such crude realism the Englishman says "nobody, somebody," i.e., никакого тела, некоторое тело, instead of никто, некто. The French language does not conceive of this peculiarity quite so sharply (although in it as well нечто is *quelque chose*), but at the same time in other instances it is much more impoverished than English. For example, it has only one word, "conscience," for the expression of two such different concepts as сознание [consciousness] and совесть [conscience], and similarly существо [creature, being] and бытие [existence, being] are rendered in French by the single word *être,* while "spirit" and "mind" are expressed by the word *esprit.* It is not surprising that in the face of such poverty of language the French did not advance in the area of philosophy further than the first elements of speculative thought established by Descartes and Malebranche; all the philosophy that succeeded them consists of echoes of

---

f. The words *actualité,* "actuality," which could correspond to действительность, *Wirklichkeit,* in general are unusable, but when they are used it is with a different connotation.

g. Besides the aforementioned example there are many others that prove this deficiency; two of them will be mentioned at this point.

others' ideas and fruitless eclecticism.[h] Likewise, the English as a consequence of the coarse realism peculiar to their intellect and expressed in their language, could elaborate only the surface of philosophical problems; for them the most profound questions of speculative thought do not seem to exist at all.

---

[h]. In this vein, Condillac was only a caricature of Locke, Saint-Martin in his most mature works is only the follower of Jacob Boehme, Maine de Biran in his own words reproduces Fichte, while other, so-called spiritualists either retell Descartes or parody Schelling and Hegel.

APPENDIX

Selected Works by V. S. Solovyov: Philosopher, Poet, and Literary Critic

Note: The works are arranged chronologically. The dates in parentheses following the titles refer to the year of completion for that work. Solovyov's writings quite often appeared in print during the same year in which he finished them.

"The Mythological Process in Ancient Paganism" (1873)
The Crisis of Western Philosophy (Against the Positivists) (1874)
"Evenings in Cairo" (1875)
"Metaphysics and Positive Science" (1875)
"Three Encounters (Moscow, London, Egypt. 1862–1875–1876). A Poem"
"The Experience of Synthetic Philosophy" (1877)
The Philosophical Principles of Integral Knowledge (1877)
Critique of Abstract Principles (1877-80)
"The White Lily: A Dream on the Night of Pokrov" (1878-80)
Lectures on Godmanhood (1877-81)
"Three Speeches in Memory of F. M. Dostoevsky" (1881-83)
Russia and the Universal Church (1883)
The Great Controversy and Christian Politics (1883)
The Spiritual Foundations of Life (1882-84)
"Judaism and the Christian Question" (1884)
The History and Future of Theocracy (1885-87)
"Russia and Europe" (1888)
"Beauty in Nature" (1889)
"Primitive Paganism, Its Surviving and Dead Remnants" (1890)
"On Lyrical Poetry. Concerning Recent Poems of Fet and Polonsky" (1890)

APPENDIX

"The Illusion of Poetic Creativity" (1890)
"The Universal Meaning of Art" (1890)
The National Question in Russia (1883-88, 1888-91)
"Byzantinism and Russia" (1891)
"On Counterfeits" (1891)
"On the Decline of the Medieval Worldview" (1891)
"Free Will and Causality" (1892-93)
"The Meaning of Love" (1892-94)
"A Buddhist Mood in Poetry" (1894)
"The Poetry of Tiutchev" (1895)
"The Poetry of A. K. Tolstoy" (1895)
"The Poetry of Ya. P. Polonsky. A Critical Essay" (1896)
Justification of the Good. Moral Philosophy (1897)
"The Fate of Pushkin" (1897)
"Plato's Life-Drama" (1898)
"The Idea of a Superman" (1899)
"A Special Celebration of Pushkin" (1899)
"The Significance of Poetry in the Verse of Pushkin" (1899)
"Three Conversations about War, Progress, and the End of World History, Including a Short Story about the Antichrist with Appendices" (1899-1900)
"Lermontov" (1900)

Notes

This unfinished work of Vladimir Solovyov represents the first draft of his extensive philosophical system. Solovyov considered this work one of his most important, and for this reason included it in the "List of Works" that he compiled in 1890 at the request of Ya. N. Kolubovsky for the third volume of Iberverg's translation of *The History of Philosophy.*

The work was first published in the *Journal of the Ministry of Public Enlightenment* in 1877 (vol. 190, no. 3, sec. II, pp. 60-99; no. 4, pp. 235-253; vol. 191, no. 6, pp. 199-233; vol. 193, no. 10, pp. 79-109; vol. 194, no. 11, pp. 1-32). The first chapter was published in an addendum to Solovyov's doctoral dissertation "Critique of Abstract Principles" (M., 1880) under the title "Concerning the Law of Historical Development."

The notes below were written by N. A. Kormin and S. L. Krawiec.

Part I

1. Material cause (Lat.); acting cause (Lat.); acting cause (Gk.); formal cause (Lat.); final cause (Lat.).

2. See V. F. Miller, *Essays on Ariisk Mythology in Connection with the Culture of Antiquity* (1876), vol. 1.

3. If you will permit me to say (Lat.).

4. From A. K. Tolstoy's poem "A Tear Trembles in Your Jealous Eyes."

5. The holy people of Rome (Lat.); the holy emperor (Lat.) — from the time of the overthrow of emperors in Rome — the high priest (pagan).

6. The sacred from the profane (Lat.).

7. *The City of God* (Lat.) — the most important work of Blessed Augustine [known to the Western world as Saint Augustine, he retains the status of "blessed" rather than "saint" in

the Christian East because of some of his doctrinal divergences from Orthodox Christianity — trans.].

8. After their condemnation at the ecumenical council in 1215, the Albigensians were annihilated in the Crusade of 1229.

9. The third estate (Fr.).

10. Officially (Lat.); in fact (Lat.).

11. See, for example, A. Gratry, *Cours de philosophie* (Paris, 1864), esp. note 10 to p. 9.

12. The lines have not yet been identified.

13. Sincere well wishes (Lat.).

14. From A. K. Tolstoy's poem "Against the Current."

15. Rabble (Lat.).

16. The lines have not yet been identified.

17. The highest good (Lat.)

Part II

1. An attitude known in advance; a prejudice (Lat.).

2. Solution to the mystery (Fr.).

3. Eternal truths and universals (Lat.).

4. The same by means of the same (Lat.). A logical error consisting of the fact that a concept that is part of what is being defined or a condition that is part of what is being proven is introduced in an unnoticeable way into a definition or a proof.

5. E. von Hartmann, *Kritische Grundlesung des transcendentalen Realismus* (Berlin, 1875).

6. By means of the same/by the same principle (Lat.).

Part III

1. For one who understands, this is enough (Lat.).

2. Nothing from nothing (Lat.).

3. Transition to another kind (Gk.) — a logical mistake, equivalence of a so-called substitution for a thesis.

4. Anticipation of a basis (Lat.) — a logical mistake consisting of a hidden assumption of an unproved premise as evidence.

5. Nature — sin (Ger.), soul — devil (Ger.).

6. Right to exist (Fr.).

7. Universals (i.e., general concepts) after things (Lat.).

8. Universals before things (Lat.).

9. A created spirit cannot penetrate the depths of nature (Ger.).

10. As an example (Lat.).

11. *Critique of Pure Reason* of Kant, *Science of Logic* of Hegel, and *System of Syllogistic and Inductive Logic* of John Mill (Moscow, 1914).

12. The existent; the existent and everything (Gk.).
13. Universal suffrage (Fr.).

Part IV

1. Of the entire sky (Lat.), i.e., of a distance from Earth to the Sun.
2. The lines have not been identified.
3. And everything strives for being, / In order to participate in being. (trans. N. Wilmont).
4. Vladimir Solovyov, "As in the pure azure of a calmed sea."
5. The lines have not been identified.
6. The first matter (Lat.).
7. Visible (Gk.).
8. *Phenomenology of the Spirit*, one of the most important works by Hegel (see: *Coll. Works*, Moscow, 1959, vol. 4).
9. *Phenomenology of the Spirit*, 51-71.
10. Feeling is everything (Ger.); feeling is nothing (Ger.).
11. Matter; nonbeing (Gk.).
12. If one can compare the great with the small (Lat.).
13. For a start (Gk.).
14. Logos existing in God or issuing from God (Gk.) — the term of Philo of Alexandria. In the given context most likely: the internal logos or revealed logos (Gk.).
15. Second matter (Lat.) — the term of John Duns Scotus.

Part V

1. Focus, center (Lat.).
2. Philosophy of identity (Lat.).
3. Identity of the indistinguishable — a logical law introduced by Leibnitz.
4. Reduction to absurdity (Lat.).
5. Absolute limit — one of the most important terms of Fichte.
6. At night all cats are gray (Fr.).

Index

absolute, the, 139-43, 150-52
absolute beauty, 145-46
absolute-being-in-itself, 163
absolute content, 50
absolute existent, 102, 121, 140
absolute first principle, 71, 97-104, 113, 116, 119, 131, 139
absolute good, 145
absolutely-existent, 110, 111, 112, 116, 121, 122, 125, 126, 134, 140-41, 163
absolute potential, 151
absolute principle, 73, 88, 97, 101, 103, 111, 136
absolute thought, 145 note a
absolute unity, 146
act, the, 142, 150, 152-54
Albigensians, 38
Anaximander, 60
Aphrodite, 48
Aristotle, 105
atheism, 48
atomism, 49
atoms, 61-63
Augustine, 36
  De civitate Dei, 36

Bacon, Francis, 77
beauty, 30-32, 46, 69, 110, 127-33, 135-37, 141-44

being, 24, 50, 62, 80, 93, 96-100, 104, 105, 109, 111-13, 115, 116, 118, 120-25, 128, 129, 131, 135-36, 140-43, 146, 149, 150, 152, 155, 157 note c, 164, 167
  absolute, 67
  empirical, 101, 102, 144
  first principles of, 164
  ideal, 96
  in-itself, 106, 160, 163
  logical, 157
  material, 67, 167
  metaphysical, 90, 92, 93
  modes of, 128-30, 135-36, 148, 149, 154
  objective, 96, 126, 134
  origin of, 98
  phenomenal, 89
  physical, 81
  pure, 67, 106
  real, 96
  spiritual, 70
  subjective, 96, 123, 126
  thirst for, 134
Berkeley, George, 160
Biran, Maine de, 168 note h
body, 163
Boehme, Jacob, 168 note h
Bogomilism, 38
Bruno, Giordano, 60
Buddhism, philosophers of, 162

175

Buddhist nirvana, 77

Catharism, 38
Catholic Church (Roman Church), 23, 37, 38-39, 43
Catholicism, 37
cause, 158-60, 163, 164
Celts-Slavs, 38-39
Charlemagne, 38
Christianity, 35-37, 49
    Christ, 37, 38
    God the Father, 139, 140
    Holy Spirit, 122, 127, 136, 139, 141
    Son, the, 139
    Trinity, doctrine of, 127
    Trinity, supreme, superessential, 140
    Western, 48
civilization, Western, 43, 46-49
cognition, 45, 53, 58, 59, 63, 65, 69, 75, 76, 83, 84, 86, 87, 90, 91, 93-100, 102-5, 107, 109, 110, 112, 139, 146, 160, 161
    absolute, 85
    logical, 139
    metaphysical, 88, 91
communitarianism/*sobornost*, 54 note *
Condillac, Étienne, 168 note h
conscience, 167
consciousness, 20, 66, 68, 78-79, 92, 106, 124, 126, 167
    das bessere Bewusstsein, 32
Constantine the Great, 36-37
content, 136, 141-44, 148, 149-51, 153, 154, 155, 157, 161, 165-66
    personal, 165
    positive, 165

deism, 69
Descartes, René, 69, 167, 168 note h
desire, 134
development, 19-22, 24, 33, 48, 49 note o, 50-51, 53-56, 76, 78, 80, 87-88, 112, 122, 124, 127, 133, 137, 146, 151
    law of development, 19, 35, 51, 55, 146, 152

difference, 153-57
Diocletian, 36
divinity, 163, 164
Divinity, 143, 160
dualism, 164

effect, 158-60, 163, 164
egotism, 165
Eleatic School, 105
element, 22-23, 33, 50, 60, 96, 102, 103, 104, 109, 110, 126 note h, 135, 145, 146, 149-50, 152
empiricism, 62-66, 68, 69, 71, 72, 76, 86, 95, 102, 142
    external, 59
    naturalistic, 96
En-Sof, 113 note b, 115, 122, 124 note f, 136, 139
entity, 146-47, 163, 166
essence, 87, 88, 100, 105, 109, 115, 117, 120, 121, 123-26, 128, 131-33, 135-37, 140-44, 146, 149, 152, 153, 157, 163
    metaphysical, 91, 92, 136
eternal Father, 122 note c
eternal Son, 122 note c
ethics, 107
existence, 19, 33, 63, 80, 82, 92, 100, 113, 119, 123, 124, 140-42, 149, 153-54, 166, 167
    absolute, 26
    forms of, 163
    human, 29
    lawful, 26
    material, 26, 105, 117, 167
    purpose of, 19
    question of, 19
existent, 70, 76, 86, 89, 90, 91, 93, 96-99, 101, 104-7, 109, 111, 119-20, 122-32, 134, 135-36, 140-44, 146, 148, 152, 155-57, 160-63
    as it appears, 163
    in-itself, 160, 161, 163
    subjects of existent ("spirit," "mind," "soul"), 130-31, 142-43

Index

experience, 78, 87-88, 95

feeling, 109, 110, 112, 113, 125, 126, 128-33, 135-36, 141-43, 148, 149, 154
Fichte, Johann Gottlieb, 160, 162, 168 note h
fine art, 30
first principle, 60, 101
form, 136, 141-43, 145, 148, 149, 152-57, 160-63, 164-68
freedom, 77-79, 114-16, 118, 129, 134
free unity, 33
French Revolution, 40-42

Germanic conquerors, 37
God, 35-36, 110, 114, 117, 120, 121, 123, 136, 139
good, the, 127-33, 135-37, 141-44
Gorgy, M., 105
Gratry, Abbott, 45

Hartmann, E. von, 32
   Grundlesung des transcendentales Realismus, 68
Heckel, Johann Jakob, 110 note a
Hegel, G. W. F., 24 note a, 29, 45, 55, 67, 73, 94-95, 105, 106, 113 note b, 123 note e, 145 note a, 155-58, 162, 163, 168 note h
   abstract rationalism, 158
   an sich/in-itself, 157, 160
   dialectics, 104-5, 107, 150, 155, 157
   Hegelianism, 45, 68 note a, 73 note e, 81, 156
   Phänomenologie des Geistes, 123 note e
   thesis/antithesis/synthesis, 147
   über das Wesen, 162
   Die Wissenschaft der Logik, 95
historical development, 24-25
history, 20, 51, 54, 80
Holy Germanic-Roman Empire, 38
hylozoism, 60

idea, 76, 82-86, 95, 98, 103, 104, 112, 119-20, 127, 129, 132, 134-37, 139-51, 156, 159, 160, 163-66
idealism, 67, 68 note a, 92
   rationalistic, 96
   subjective, 158, 160
ideals, abstract, 165
identity, 152, 153, 156, 157
   law of, 152, 153, 155, 157, 158
imagination, 58, 126-33, 135-36, 141-43, 145, 148, 149
indefinite potential, 151
integral knowledge, 53, 56, 57, 71-73, 75-76, 78, 86-87, 101, 109, 111, 151
integral society, 54
intellectual currents, 45
   empirical, 45
   rationalist, 45
intellektuelle Anschauung (intuition), 82
Ionian School, 60
Islam, 37
   Islamic East, 49
Israelites, 37

Justinian, 36

Kabbalists, 113 note b
Kant, I., 67, 69 note *, 92, 94, 95, 110, 160-63
   Ding an sich/thing-in-itself, 88, 89, 158-63
   Kritik der reinen Vernunft, 95
   transcendental aesthetics, 162
knowledge, 27-28, 45, 50, 56, 57, 60, 69, 71, 77, 79, 87, 92, 94, 95, 109, 110, 123
   human, 163
   metaphysical, 88, 90
Kraft und Stoff, 61

language/languages, 166-68
Locke, John, 168 note h
logic, 150, 165
   circular, 165
   principle of, 150

INDEX

logical categories, 152, 156, 157, 160
  correlative characteristics, the one and the many, 154, 157
  correlative characteristics, unconditional and relative, 154-55, 157
  other, the, 140, 147, 149-50, 153-59, 161
  same, the, 140, 147, 149-50, 153-59
  something, 147-51, 158-59, 164, 167
Logos, 109, 113, 121-25, 127, 128, 131, 134, 135-36, 139-46
  absolute, 152, 154
  embodied or concrete, 140
  internal or concealed, 139-41
  law of, 130
  real or revealed, 140-41
Louis XIV, 43
love, 114, 117, 131
Ludwig XIV, 45

magic, 140
Malebranche, Nicolas de, 167
Mammon, 110
materialism, 61-62
  elemental, 60
  mechanical, 61, 63
matter, 62-63, 114, 117-20, 124, 125, 131, 133-36, 140, 145, 164-68
Maya, 140
metaphysics, 48, 87, 88, 107, 163
  systems of, 100
Middle Ages, 23, 37-39, 44, 46, 53
might, 120
Mill, J. S., 95
  The System of Logic, 95
Miller, V. F., 25 note b
mind, 130-33, 135-37, 141-46, 149, 150, 152, 156, 157, 164, 167
  Original Mind, 144-45, 152, 154
monism, 49, 163
monologism, 163
multiplicity, 54
mysticism, 31-32, 46, 48, 53, 69, 70-72, 76, 81

naturalism, 59-63, 67
  empirical, 68
nature, 120-22, 123, 127, 130, 131, 136, 143, 163, 164
necessity, 120
Nicozisin, Fr. George, 38
nonbeing, 150
nothing (as concept), 157 note c, 159, 167

Old Testament, 37
organic logic, 73, 75, 93, 97, 98, 101, 102, 104-5, 109, 139, 146, 150, 155
organism, 20-24, 32, 52, 55, 80, 130, 146, 152
Origen, 36
Orthodox Christianity (Eastern Church), 37, 54 note *

paganism, 36
Parmenedes, 151
person, definition of, 83
  as category, 146
phenomenon/phenomena, 49, 60-64, 65, 66, 70, 79, 80-82, 84, 86, 88-93, 96, 99 note b, 103, 109-11, 144, 158-64
  in-itself, 163
philosophy, 107, 110, 113, 118, 153, 155-58, 160, 162, 167
  academic, 59, 67, 71, 87, 95, 97, 103, 120, 151, 161
  alpha and omega of, 151
  definition of, 58-59
  empirical, 71
  end of, 151
  European, 162
  formal, 155
  metaphysical, 163
  naturalistic, 60-61
  origin of, 150-51
  principle of, 150
  rationalist, 111-12
  scholastic, 69, 84
  speculative, 150, 167
  subject of, 59, 85, 96-97

Index

superficial, 162
task of, 103, 150
three types of, 57-73
Western, 101
Plato, 53 note *, 105
poetry, 46
positivism, 45-47
Protestantism, 39
proto-god, 140

rationalism, 71, 72, 76, 94, 95, 102
realism, 47, 167, 168
reality, 94-97, 101-3, 105, 106, 112, 113, 117, 121, 122, 127, 129, 134-36, 145, 149-51, 155-59, 165-67
   empirical, 126
   material, 167
reason, 92, 101-4, 106, 109, 112
relativity, 101
religion, 32, 34 note g, 48, 77, 100-101
   Jewish religion, 38
   positive religions, 165
Renaissance, 44, 46
Roman laws, 36-37
Roman-Byzantine government, 36-37
Russia, 38
   nation of, 51
   people of, 51, 54

Saint-Martin, Louis Claude de, 168 note h
Schelling, F. W. J. von, 145, 150, 162, 168 note h
Identitätsphilosophie, 150
scholasticism, 44, 83
   scholastics, 64
Schopenhauer, A., 32, 127, 156
science, 156, 163
   positive, 163
skepticism, 69 note *, 87, 88, 95, 102, 103, 105
Slavic peoples, 51
social ideals, 165
socialism, 43, 45-47, 54 note r

Sophia, 140
soul, 130-33, 135-36, 141-43, 149, 156, 163, 164
speculative thought, 168
Spencer, Herbert, 24 note a
spirit, 130, 132-36, 141-43, 149, 156, 163, 164, 167
superexistent, 115, 118, 120, 139, 141, 150, 157 note c
   superexistent absolute, 139, 151
   superexistent principle as such, 142

theocracy, 34, 54, 55 note *, 56, 78
   free theocracy, 53-54, 56
Theodosius I, 36
theosophy, 34, 55 note *, 56, 73, 75, 104
   free theosophy, 53, 57, 71-72, 76, 78, 82, 86, 87, 93
   free theurgy, 56
theurgy, 34, 55 note *, 56
three basic forms of being, 25
   active will/objective good, 25, 54
   feeling/objective beauty, 25, 54, 58
   thinking/objective truth, 25, 54
truly-existent, 60, 67-68, 76-78, 86, 88, 89, 93, 100, 103
truth, 56, 69-70, 94, 98, 100, 102, 109-10, 127-33, 135-37, 141-47, 151, 155-59, 161
   integral truth, 57, 82
   metaphysical truth, 88
   one-sided, 158

unity, 54, 98, 100, 101, 113-16, 131, 132, 139, 142-50, 152-56, 158, 159, 164-66
   absolute unities, 137
   principle of, 165
   social, 165
universal goal of humankind, 20

will, 58, 109, 110, 112, 123, 124, 126-36, 141-43, 145, 148, 149, 154
wisdom, 58
Wolff, Christian, 69 note *
Word, the, 123

www.ingramcontent.com/pod-product-compliance
Lightning Source LLC
Chambersburg PA
CBHW021830300426
44114CB00009BA/386